the
comfortable
kitchen

the comfortable kitchen

kitchen

105 LAID-BACK, HEALTHY, AND WHOLESOME RECIPES

ALEX SNODGRASS

PHOTOGRAPHY BY KRISTEN KILPATRICK

WILLIAM MORROW

An Imprint of HarperCollinsPublishers

To Sutton and Winnie:
May we continue to make
memories in
the kitchen together
for you to carry in your
hearts forever.

contents

introduction

When I was trying to decide what types of recipes to include in this book, I thought long and hard about my experience writing my first cookbook and putting it out into the world. Sharing that with the Defined Dish community for the first time was incredibly daunting yet exciting, and one of the most profoundly rewarding experiences of my life thus far. All I wanted was for people to actually cook and enjoy the recipes with the ones they love most—not just a little memento that collects dust on a shelf.

While I love to treat my body well and eat foods that nourish, food is also so much more than just what fuels our bodies. Meals are where our families come together at the end of the day. They're where we celebrate life's great events. They're where we gather and count our blessings. And they're where we can show others that we love and care about them.

Food has always been my love language. More specifically, preparing and serving food. In fact, when I really dig deep, food is the love language that has shaped so many of my relationships and continues to.

The bulk of my childhood memories are set in the kitchen: my dad, mom, brother, and sister around the table eating my mom's delicious meals. I know now that I, too, can set the foundation for beautiful memories made at home for our little family of four.

I express my own motherly love through my cooking for my two beautiful children. Sure, right now they may be more interested in the fast food we eat on occasion, and sometimes have the gumption to request something else for dinner; however, one day I know they'll look back and remember The Best Bolognese (page 82) that I like to make on special occasions and be filled with warm memories of our family together in the kitchen.

Whipping up my husband's favorite Perfectly Broiled Rib Eye with Tarragon Butter (page 130) makes my heart so happy. I love nothing more than a date night in, a lovely bottle of wine, and catching up on our week together over a delicious home-cooked meal. The meals I make are a labor of love, and a way that I show him I care.

And, true friendship to me is writing notes on top of a foil-wrapped casserole dish filled with my Eggplant Lasagna (page 94) and leaving it at the front porch of a dear friend or family member in need of a home-cooked meal. Whenever I'm on the receiving end of a delicious delivered dinner from a friend, I'm always grateful for the time and love put forth into making sure I'm fed and comforted.

Long story long—preparing, sharing, and serving food for others brings me joy, which is exactly what brings me to writing my second book. I feel like it's my purpose in life to share this passion with you, and I can't wait for you to quite literally dig into the recipes here.

My intention with this book—and all of the recipes I create—is to bring you into my kitchen with me, in the hope that I can bring a little more comfort into yours. Even if you love cooking as much as I do, it can feel like you are in this constant cycle of cooking, scrubbing pots and pans, and filling the dishwasher, only to get up and do it all over again—I get it. But even when we are stuck in this constant cycle, how can we remind ourselves about the joy cooking can bring us, and how it makes such a positive impact on the way we feel? How can we get creative in our kitchens without worrying about overcooking our chicken? How can we put food on the table that's somewhat healthy and still makes our taste buds sing and fill our loved ones with comfort?

That's where I want to help—to inspire you with delicious food that doesn't skimp on flavor. Let me remind you, I'm just a home cook who loves sharing recipes, so you'll find my recipes are easy enough that any and all levels of cook will love and enjoy. I'm also not a dietician. I'm just a human being doing my best to live a healthy and abundant life. While most of these recipes are created with clean, healthful ingredients, there are a handful of splurge-worthy dishes in here—like my Fried Mortadella Sandwiches (page 123)—because, in my opinion, life is too short, and we should enjoy a little bit of everything if we are able.

You'll find that in this book I've stuck to what I do best—great dinners for all occasions and for all levels of difficulty: busy weeknight dinners, weekend dinners with friends, and family-style dinners for special moments. I've also included some accompaniments to add to your dinner experience. The Clayton's Cocktails chapter (page 227) has some fun spirited beverages to pair with dinner or kick off a lovely evening. The cocktails can be perfectly paired with the appetizer chapter (page 10), which is filled with bites and dips for grazing before dinner or a festive happy hour with friends. And last—and if you're a long-time follower, you may not believe me when I say this—there is a Something Sweet chapter (page 213), with desserts I'm extremely proud of and excited for you to try.

At the end of the day, food is a powerful way of expressing love and forming deeper connections, and my hope is that as you cook your way through this book, you'll take the time to appreciate the way that food brings us all together.

pantry staples

FLOURS

ALMOND FLOUR

This has been a tried-and-true staple in my pantry for many years. While it's great for grain-free baking, it's also terrific for savory cooking when I want to try to mimic bread crumbs or panko. I don't recommend using almond flour as a thickener in sauces and gravies —I have other options for that—as it can create a gritty texture and it doesn't thicken like all-purpose flour; however, it's great at binding to foods to create a crispy breading!

CASSAVA FLOUR

For grain-free and gluten-free cooking, cassava gets close to being the ultimate replacement for all-purpose flour. It is very mild and neutral in flavor, light and fine, and not grainy or gritty in texture. The other thing about cassava is that it is nut-free, making it a good substitute for those with nut allergies who cannot use almond flour. In savory cooking, you can usually swap cassava flour for all-purpose flour using a 1:1 ratio; in baking, it can get a little more cumbersome as it absorbs liquid more easily than all-purpose flour.

ARROWROOT FLOUR/STARCH

Some call it arrowroot starch and some call it arrowroot flour— it's all the same thing! This powdery white starch is naturally gluten-free, grain-free, paleo, and Whole30-friendly. However, beware that some lower-quality arrowroot flour blends may also contain potato starch, which is why I like to buy Bob's Red Mill brand. Arrowroot is more similar to cornstarch in cooking than it is to all-purpose flour. Like cornstarch, arrowroot is excellent for thickening soups, sauces, and gravies. It does have a very strong thickening power, so a little goes a long way—or else your food can get too thick or slimy.

TAPIOCA FLOUR/STARCH

Tapioca is a starch extracted from the yuca root and, like arrowroot flour, it is a powdery white starch that is naturally gluten-free, grain-free, paleo, and Whole30-friendly and it can serve as a substitute in cooking and baking. Because tapioca flour is super similar to arrowroot flour, it can usually be used interchangeably in my recipes, as it is excellent for thickening soups, sauces, and gravies. The only difference I do notice with tapioca is that when it is combined with almond flour, it tends to lend a crispier breading than arrowroot.

DAIRY-FREE MILKS

DAIRY-FREE CREAMER

I use this probably every single day. From my morning coffee to creaming up a delicious pot of soup for dinner, it really is a secret weapon in the kitchen. If you're okay with dairy, you can sub in heavy cream where I call for dairy-free creamer, but I always try to keep an unflavored dairy-free creamer on hand, and my current favorite brand is nutpods Original Almond + Coconut Creamer. I also recommend bringing it to room temperature before using it in hot dishes, as it is less likely to curdle. Since most dairy-free creamers are nut based, if you need a nut-free option, you can use coconut milk in the recipes where I call for dairy-free creamer.

COCONUT MILK

Unsweetened full-fat, always! This will ensure the best texture and creaminess when cooking. It's obviously wonderful when making Asian-inspired dishes like Creamy Cauliflower Green Curry Soup (page 54), but it's also a great sub for heavy creamer in other savory cooking recipes like Steak au Poivre (page 112). Do note that some brands have a more distinct coconut flavor than others; I find Aroyo or Thai Kitchen brands to be the mildest.

OILS

AVOCADO OIL

Avocado oil is neutral in flavor and is a must-have pantry staple. I use it to make homemade mayonnaise (page 251), bake sweets, and cook many of my savory recipes. Avocado oil has a higher smoke point than olive oil, meaning that it doesn't burn as quickly, so I tend to use avocado oil for cooking techniques that require high temperatures, such as sautéing, grilling, and searing.

EXTRA-VIRGIN OLIVE OIL

A good, delicious extra-virgin olive oil can go a long way in the kitchen, from making simple side salads to drizzling over fresh summer tomatoes, and it's also just fine for low- to medium-temperature cooking!

BROTHS AND FLAVORINGS

LOW-SODIUM CHICKEN OR VEGETABLE BROTH

This one may seem obvious and something you already keep in your pantry. So let this just be a reminder of how useful broth can be in cooking. Not only is it essential for soup but it can also be used to rehydrate ground meat or rice and add flavor without watering down the recipe.

COCONUT AMINOS

Coconut aminos is a salty, savory liquid seasoning made from the fermented sap of the coconut palm and sea salt. Coconut aminos has a color and consistency similar to soy sauce, making it an easy substitute in paleo and Whole30 cooking, since soy is not a compatible ingredient in those styles of cooking. It does have a sweeter flavor than soy sauce, so I typically pair it with fish sauce when cooking Asian-inspired dishes. Also, be sure to use coconut aminos—not liquid aminos, which will leave you with a much saltier dish, as they are not the same!

DIJON MUSTARD

Whether you're a mustard fan or not, it's time to start cooking with Dijon mustard as it adds an abundance of flavor. It's great to thicken up and add flavor to any salad dressing, but it also works as an emulsifier in a pan sauce that starts with the drippings rendered from cooking meat. Its flavor pairs well with everything from chicken to steak, and it's one of the easiest ingredients to keep on hand to make any weeknight dinner feel a little more special.

FISH SAUCE

Few ingredients bring as much immediate, showstopping flavor to a dish as fish sauce; it adds a burst of umami and saltiness to any recipe. Although it's most commonly used in Asian cooking, it can be used in salad dressings and marinades to take the flavor up a notch. I love Red Boat brand, as it has no added sugar and is gluten-free.

TOMATO PASTE

Tomato paste is basically super-concentrated tomato sauce. The benefit of using tomato paste over other canned tomatoes (like tomato puree, crushed tomatoes, or diced tomatoes), or even fresh tomatoes, is that you get the deep tomato flavor without all the extra water, making it great for recipes in which you don't want a ton of liquid.

SWEETENERS

COCONUT SUGAR

For paleo baking and cooking, I love using coconut sugar as an alternative to cane sugar and brown sugar. While coconut sugar *is still sugar*, it can be viewed as a healthier alternative to refined sugar. Coconut sugar has a lower glycemic index ranking than cane sugar. I also love coconut sugar's mild caramel flavor, which rounds out baked goods with a slight earthiness. It's also great to add a touch of sweetness to savory-acidic recipes like Tender Oven-Baked Ribs with Vinegary BBQ Sauce (page 137) to help balance out the flavors.

HONEY

Honey is another great alternative to refined sugar, especially when used in baking sweets. I always keep some on hand to add a touch of sweetness where needed, like in salad dressings and sauces. I also use honey as a substitute for corn syrup in my Scotcharoos (page 214), which you just have to try, the recipe's a family favorite.

MAPLE SYRUP

Thinking beyond refined sugars, 100% pure maple syrup is a less processed liquid sweetener packed with a complex, layered flavor that's perfect for baking. It can work well in any recipe that's lightly sweetened and in baked goods like my 7-Ingredient Almond Butter Cookies (page 223) and Birthday Cake Blondies (page 224).

appetizers

Paleo Pigs in a Blanket

MAKES ABOUT 24 • TOTAL TIME: 30 MINUTES

Is there really a better appetizer than a pig in a blanket? These bite-size, baked snacks appeal to kids and adults alike. Whether you're at a potluck dinner or a fancy cocktail party, you know this will be one of the first items to disappear! I'm not going to lie—it took me about twenty tries to get a paleo version of them right. But I was determined to make it happen! So, roll them up, toss them in the oven, kick back with a drink in hand, and enjoy the party!

1 large egg

2 tablespoons avocado oil

1 teaspoon honey

⅔ cup plus 1 tablespoon almond flour

⅓ cup plus 2 tablespoons tapioca flour

¼ teaspoon baking powder

¼ teaspoon kosher salt

One 12-ounce package smoked cocktail sausages

Spicy brown mustard and/or ketchup (I like Primal Kitchen brand), optional for dipping

FROM MY KITCHEN TO YOURS

These can be made ahead for an easy, delicious appetizer. I suggest freezing them before baking. Freeze the prepared pigs in a blanket on a parchment-lined sheet pan. When they are completely frozen (which takes 3 to 4 hours), transfer them to a freezer-safe zip-top bag. They keep well in the freezer for up to 3 months. To bake from frozen, preheat the oven to 350°F and bake on a parchment-lined sheet pan for 15 to 17 minutes.

PREHEAT the oven to 350°F. Line a sheet pan with parchment paper.

IN a large bowl, whisk together the egg, oil, and honey until well combined. Add ⅔ cup of the almond flour, ⅓ cup of the tapioca flour, the baking powder, and salt. Using a rubber spatula, stir until very well combined. Add 1 tablespoon of the tapioca flour and the remaining 1 tablespoon almond flour and use the rubber spatula to stir until well combined. The dough should be starting to come together as a ball. Sprinkle the remaining 1 tablespoon tapioca flour over the ball of dough and, using your hands, work the flour until it is well combined with the dough mixture.

BECAUSE paleo dough can be sticky and difficult to work with, you will need two sheets of parchment paper (about 12 inches long) to roll it out. Place one sheet of parchment paper on the counter and place the dough in the center. Top with the second sheet of parchment paper and use a rolling pin to roll the dough into a large rectangle about 9 × 12 inches and about ⅛ inch thick (the thickness is more important than the other dimensions). Carefully remove the top sheet of parchment paper.

USING a pizza cutter or paring knife, cut the dough down the center lengthwise. Then, cut the dough crosswise into long triangles about 1½ inches across at the wide end. Next, place one of the cocktail sausages on the wide end one of the triangles and gently roll to wrap. Place on the prepared sheet pan. Repeat to wrap the rest of the sausages, placing them 1 inch apart on the pan.

BAKE until golden brown, 8 to 12 minutes.

SERVE with your favorite dipping sauce and enjoy!

Chorizo-Stuffed Bacon-Wrapped Dates

GLUTEN-FREE
DAIRY-FREE
PALEO
WHOLE30
GRAIN-FREE

MAKES 4 SERVINGS • TOTAL TIME: 45 MINUTES

Here's an appetizer you're going to love sinking your teeth into! Inspired by AVEC restaurant in Chicago, this appetizer stuffs delicious, flavorful chorizo into sweet dates that are then wrapped with crispy, salty bacon. Served over a creamy roasted red pepper sauce, these little bites will wow your guests and your taste buds!

FOR THE ROASTED RED PEPPER SAUCE

2 tablespoons extra-virgin olive oil

¼ cup minced shallot (about 1 large shallot)

2 garlic cloves, minced

Pinch of kosher salt

A few cracks of black pepper

1 cup roughly chopped jarred roasted red peppers

2 tablespoons liquid from the jar of roasted peppers

One 14.5-ounce can whole peeled tomatoes

1 tablespoon sherry vinegar

FOR THE STUFFED DATES

16 pitted Medjool dates

8 ounces fresh chorizo, bulk or casings removed (I use San Manuel chorizo; see note)

8 slices bacon, halved lengthwise (I use Applegate no-sugar bacon)

1 tablespoon finely chopped fresh parsley, for serving

PAIRING SUGGESTION: **Whiskey Sour** (page 241)

PREHEAT the oven to 350°F. Line a sheet pan with parchment paper.

MAKE THE ROASTED RED PEPPER SAUCE: In a small saucepan, heat the oil over medium heat. Add the shallot, garlic, salt, and black pepper and cook, stirring often, until tender, 2 to 3 minutes. Add the roasted peppers, the liquid from the jar, the tomatoes, and the vinegar and bring to a rapid simmer. Reduce the heat to low, cover, and simmer while you bake the dates to allow the flavors to meld.

PREPARE THE STUFFED DATES: Gently open up a date so that it can easily be stuffed. Place about ½ tablespoon of the chorizo in the cavity of the date. Wrap with a half-strip of bacon and secure with a toothpick. Place on the lined sheet pan and repeat to stuff the rest of the dates.

BAKE the dates until the chorizo is cooked through, 12 to 15 minutes. Turn the oven to high broil and broil until the bacon is just crisp, 2 to 4 minutes, depending on your broiler.

MEANWHILE, carefully transfer the sauce to a blender and blend until smooth and creamy. Return to the saucepan, cover, and keep warm until the dates are done.

TO SERVE: Spoon and spread about one-third of the pepper sauce (see note) across a serving platter. Place the dates on top and garnish with the parsley.

FROM MY KITCHEN TO YOURS

FOR THE CHORIZO: Make sure to buy fresh (uncured) chorizo sausage rather than the salami-like cured kind.

FOR THE SAUCE: The sauce recipe makes more than you'll need for 16 dates. You can at least triple the date portion of the recipe and keep the sauce the same or (as I like to do) freeze the leftover sauce so you can whip up the bacon-wrapped dates in no time when you have a craving or are entertaining guests.

Sileo Celery Salad with Charcuterie

MAKES 6 SERVINGS • TOTAL TIME: 15 MINUTES

Named after my mom's side of the family (Sileo was her maiden name), this celery salad has been in my family for generations and generations. When I was growing up, there was never a Sileo family gathering without this celery salad as part of our antipasti platter. It's an easy-to-make element to really kick up your classic meat and cheese platter and wow your guests with something crunchy, delicious, and unique! You can really get creative with how you'd like to serve this on your platter. As a child, I'd take a big slice of provolone cheese, lay a few slices of salami on top, put a little celery salad in the middle, then fold it and eat it like a taco. Do it, trust me. You can also reserve the leftovers to throw on top of big salads. It's one of those things that gets better with time as it continues to marinate in the fridge!

8 to 10 large celery stalks

4 garlic cloves, peeled

1 cup roughly chopped drained jarred pepperoncini

⅓ cup finely minced drained jarred roasted red pepper

¼ teaspoon freshly ground black pepper, plus more to taste

2 teaspoons extra-virgin olive oil

¼ teaspoon kosher salt, plus more to taste

2 tablespoons red wine vinegar

OPTIONAL FOR SERVING

Sliced salami, mortadella, or capicola

Sliced provolone cheese

Marinated artichokes

Castelvetrano olives

TRIM the ends of the celery. Using a potato peeler, peel the outer layer of celery to remove the stringy bits. Rinse and dry the celery. Halve the stalks lengthwise, then dice. Place the diced celery in a large bowl.

STICK a toothpick into each of the garlic cloves (this makes them easy to find and remove when serving). Place the cloves in the bowl with the celery.

ADD the pepperoncini, roasted pepper, and black pepper and toss to combine. Add the olive oil and toss, then add the salt and toss again. Add the vinegar and toss once more. *(I know, it seems odd to do it in this order and not all at once, but the Sileo family swears by it, so just trust us, okay?)*

REFRIGERATE for at least 2 hours before serving—but it's best the next day. Taste and add more salt and pepper, if desired. Remove the garlic cloves to serve. You can serve chilled or at room temperature.

FROM MY KITCHEN TO YOURS

My mom usually makes this the day before a party. It keeps for 5 to 7 days in the fridge.

Crispy Smashed Potatoes with Dynamite Sauce

GLUTEN-FREE
DAIRY-FREE
PALEO
WHOLE30
GRAIN-FREE

MAKES 6 SERVINGS • TOTAL TIME: 50 MINUTES

This fun appetizer could have easily gone in the sides chapter. Would you look at those crisp, golden potatoes? Tell me you don't just want to eat the whole platter yourself! Crispy potatoes are one of those things in life that I can't get enough of, and most people feel the same way, because frankly, potatoes are the best. Paired with this zingy dynamite sauce—which you'll want to dip everything in, and you should—these crispy little potatoes will be devoured by your guests.

FOR THE POTATOES

1½ pounds baby Dutch yellow potatoes

3 tablespoons avocado oil

1 teaspoon kosher salt

½ teaspoon freshly ground black pepper

FOR THE DYNAMITE SAUCE

½ cup Homemade Mayo (page 251)

2 garlic cloves, minced

1 tablespoon freshly squeezed lemon juice (about ½ lemon)

1 tablespoon sriracha (I use Yellowbird brand)

1 teaspoon fish sauce

½ teaspoon onion powder

2 tablespoons finely chopped fresh chives, plus more for garnish

PAIRING SUGGESTIONS: **Golden Hour (page 242), Whiskey Sour (page 241)**

PREHEAT the oven to 375°F. Line a sheet pan with parchment paper.

PREPARE THE POTATOES: Place the potatoes on the lined sheet pan and drizzle with the avocado oil, salt, and pepper. Toss to coat the potatoes evenly.

BAKE until golden brown and the skin is slightly crisp, about 35 minutes, tossing halfway through.

USING a potato masher or serving fork, smash each potato to about a ¼-inch thickness. Return to the oven and bake until the edges are crispy, 10 minutes.

MAKE THE DYNAMITE SAUCE: In a small bowl or screw-top jar, combine the mayo, garlic, lemon juice, sriracha, fish sauce, onion powder, and the 2 tablespoons chives and stir until well combined. (This keeps well refrigerated for 5 to 7 days.)

SERVE the crispy potatoes with the dynamite sauce for dipping. Garnish with chives, if desired.

GLUTEN-FREE
DAIRY-FREE
PALEO
WHOLE30
GRAIN-FREE

Shrimp Ceviche

MAKES 4 SERVINGS • TOTAL TIME: 1 HOUR 15 MINUTES

This ceviche is one of my favorite appetizers to make ahead when hosting guests on a sunny day. It's bright, beautiful, and has fabulous flavor. Now, if you've never made ceviche before, yes, you chop the shrimp up raw and it does actually "cook" from the acidity of the lime juice! While this appetizer is great for any occasion, it's an especially wonderful way to cool off in the warmer summer months alongside an ice-cold Clayton's Margarita (page 230).

1 pound shrimp (31/40 count), peeled, deveined, and tails off

½ cup freshly squeezed lime juice (about 4 limes)

2 tablespoons freshly squeezed lemon juice (about 1 lemon)

3 serrano peppers, 2 halved and seeded, 1 minced (see note)

⅓ cup finely minced red onion

¼ cup finely chopped fresh cilantro

⅓ cup small-diced seeded English cucumber

½ teaspoon dried oregano

½ teaspoon kosher salt, plus more to taste

¼ teaspoon freshly ground black pepper, plus more to taste

1 avocado, cut into small dice

Grain-free chips (I use Siete Foods brand), optional for serving (omit for Whole30)

PAIRING SUGGESTIONS: Clayton's Margarita (page 230), Mezcal Mule (page 234)

CUT each shrimp in half horizontally, then cut each half into 3 or 4 smaller pieces (depending on how chunky you want your ceviche).

IN a food processor, combine the lime juice, the lemon juice, and the 2 halved serrano peppers. Blend until smooth.

PLACE the shrimp in a large bowl. Add the citrus/serrano mixture, red onion, cilantro, minced serrano, cucumber, oregano, salt, and black pepper. Using a rubber spatula, gently toss the ceviche. Cover and refrigerate for at least 1 hour, to let the flavors meld and the shrimp to cook through from the acid in the lime juice.

BEFORE serving, gently fold in the avocado and adjust the salt and black pepper as desired.

FROM MY KITCHEN TO YOURS

If you want a milder ceviche, omit the minced serrano pepper. If you love a lot of spice like me, keep the seeds in the serrano when blending it with the citrus juices.

Olive Puffs

MAKES 30 TO 40 (DEPENDING ON THE SIZE OF THE OLIVES) • TOTAL TIME: 25 MINUTES

You'll notice I mention my mother-in-law, GoGo, a few times in this book. A great cook, she's always introducing me to new flavors and recipes that inspire me in the kitchen. Over Christmas one year, she threw some of what she called "olive puffs" in the oven for an appetizer and, as a very avid olive fan, I immediately fell in love. I've made a gluten-free and grain-free rendition of her recipe and it's perfect to pop in the oven when you have guests over as an easy yet impressive and flavorful appetizer!

¾ cup freshly shredded sharp cheddar cheese (I like Tillamook)

2 tablespoons avocado oil

1 large egg

2 teaspoons honey

⅔ cup plus 1 tablespoon almond flour

⅓ cup tapioca flour

¼ teaspoon salt

¼ teaspoon baking powder

½ teaspoon paprika

30 large or 40 small pimiento-stuffed olives, drained

PAIRING SUGGESTIONS: Thyme 75 (page 238), Golden Hour (page 242)

PREHEAT the oven to 350°F. Line a sheet pan with parchment paper.

IN a large bowl, combine the cheddar, oil, egg, and honey and mix well. Add the almond flour, tapioca flour, salt, baking powder, and paprika and stir until well combined. Using your hands, form the mixture into one large dough ball.

SCOOP about 1 teaspoon of the dough (this is for smaller olives; use more as needed depending on the size of your olives) and gently mold it around an olive until the olive is entirely covered. Place the olive on the lined sheet pan and repeat with the rest of the olives.

BAKE until golden brown, about 7 minutes. Let cool for about 5 minutes before serving.

FROM MY KITCHEN TO YOURS

To make ahead, place the unbaked olive puffs on a cookie sheet. Freeze for at least 2 hours, until firm. Then, transfer the frozen puffs to freezer bags. Seal, label, and freeze for up to 3 months. When ready to bake, preheat the oven to 350°F. Place the puffs on a parchment-lined sheet pan and bake until golden brown, 10 to 12 minutes.

Truffle Pizza

MAKES 6 SERVINGS • TOTAL TIME: 20 MINUTES

Okay, so yes, this technically could be your dinner. But this has become our go-to substantial appetizer when we have guests over. I simply grab some pizza dough from the store, throw on the cheesy truffle topping, bake until browned and bubbling, and top with arugula and prosciutto—simple as that. It's super uncomplicated but tastes elegant, thanks to the truffle oil! Throw this beauty on a wooden cutting board and watch everyone ooh and aah.

One 14-ounce ball store-bought pizza dough (use gluten-free pizza dough for gluten-free option)

2 to 4 tablespoons all-purpose flour, for dusting (use gluten-free flour for gluten-free option)

2 tablespoons extra-virgin olive oil

½ cup mascarpone cheese

½ cup ricotta cheese

1 tablespoon black truffle oil

½ teaspoon crushed red pepper flakes

1 cup shredded mozzarella cheese

1 cup baby arugula

2 ounces thinly sliced prosciutto

PREHEAT the oven to 425°F.

PRESS and stretch the dough in a circular motion into about an 8-inch round, then lay out on a flat surface dusted with flour. Use a rolling pin to roll it out to a 14-inch round. Lightly dust a sheet pan or pizza peel with flour and lay the stretched pizza dough on top. Brush the pizza dough evenly all over with the olive oil.

IN a medium bowl, combine the mascarpone, ricotta, and truffle oil and mix well. Spread the cheese mixture on the pizza dough, leaving an inch or so of dough as a border. Sprinkle with the pepper flakes and mozzarella.

BAKE until the crust is golden brown and the cheese is hot, bubbling, and slightly browned on the top, 8 to 12 minutes.

REMOVE from the oven and top with the arugula and prosciutto. Slice and serve.

Smoked Salmon Dip

MAKES 4 SERVINGS • TOTAL TIME: 15 MINUTES

GLUTEN-FREE
DAIRY-FREE
PALEO
WHOLE30
GRAIN-FREE

Wonderfully easy and delicious, this is a dip to impress. You absolutely cannot buy smoked salmon dip that tastes this good! Throw all the ingredients into a food processor and this fancy-pants dip is ready in no time. It has a lovely smoky flavor from the salmon combined with the smoked paprika, a little tang from the lemon, a dash of heat from the hot sauce, and a fabulous fresh flavor from the dill. It's perfect to make ahead of a party so that it's ready to serve when your guests arrive—and you can sit back and enjoy!

¼ cup medium-diced yellow onion

2 garlic cloves, peeled

1 pound center-cut smoked salmon

¼ cup Homemade Mayo (page 251)

1 teaspoon Dijon mustard

2 tablespoons freshly squeezed lemon juice (about 1 lemon)

½ teaspoon smoked paprika

½ teaspoon kosher salt

½ teaspoon freshly ground black pepper

¼ cup chopped fresh dill, plus more for serving

2 tablespoons capers, drained

2 teaspoons your favorite hot sauce (I use El Yucateco)

Grain-free crackers, for serving (I use Simple Mills, omit for Whole30)

Cut-up fresh vegetables, such as carrots and celery, for serving

PAIRING SUGGESTION: **Golden Hour** (page 242)

IN a food processor or blender, combine the onion and garlic and process until finely chopped. Add the salmon, mayo, mustard, lemon juice, smoked paprika, salt, pepper, dill, capers, and hot sauce. Pulse until the salmon is reduced to pea-size pieces, 10 to 20 pulses, scraping down the sides as needed. Refrigerate until ready to serve.

SERVE garnished with fresh dill and with crackers and/or fresh-cut veggies.

KEEP stored in the refrigerator for up to 5 days.

satisfying salads
and bowls

Balsamic Steak Salad with Creamy Gorgonzola Dressing

GLUTEN-FREE
GRAIN-FREE

MAKES 4 SERVINGS • TOTAL TIME: 40 MINUTES

This is one of those salads that I'll cook forever. The seared steak is just so delicious, on a bed of crunchy greens for that oh-so-necessary veggie serving, and the Gorgonzola dressing . . . wow! The tangy, creamy, and robust flavor is impressive enough to serve at a dinner party. I love putting my husband on steak duty while I prepare the Gorgonzola dressing and assemble the salad. It all comes together quickly so we can enjoy our time with guests and they can be wowed by our delicious dinner.

FOR THE BALSAMIC STEAK

3 tablespoons extra-virgin olive oil

2 tablespoons balsamic vinegar

1 tablespoon Dijon mustard

1½ teaspoons kosher salt

1 teaspoon freshly ground black pepper

3 sirloin steak filets (8 ounces each)

FOR THE CREAMY GORGONZOLA DRESSING

¾ cup crumbled Gorgonzola cheese

2 garlic cloves, peeled

¼ cup extra-virgin olive oil

1 teaspoon Dijon mustard

3 tablespoons champagne vinegar

2 tablespoons freshly squeezed lemon juice (about 1 lemon)

2 tablespoons honey

¼ teaspoon kosher salt

½ teaspoon freshly ground black pepper

FOR THE SALAD

4 cups baby arugula (about one 5-ounce container)

4 cups baby spring mix (about one 5-ounce container)

¾ cup halved cherry tomatoes

½ cup thinly sliced radishes

¼ cup crumbled Gorgonzola cheese

PREPARE THE BALSAMIC STEAK: In a small bowl, whisk together the olive oil, balsamic vinegar, mustard, salt, and pepper. Pour the mixture into a large plastic bag, place the steaks in the bag, and seal. Toss the contents in the bag until the steaks are well coated. Set aside and let marinate at room temperature for 15 minutes. (Alternatively, you can marinate in the fridge for up to 24 hours in advance.)

MAKE THE CREAMY GORGONZOLA DRESSING: In a food processor or blender, combine the Gorgonzola, garlic, olive oil, mustard, champagne vinegar, lemon juice, honey, salt, and pepper. Blend on medium-low until smooth, about 1 minute. Set aside.

ASSEMBLE THE SALAD: On a large platter or in a bowl, combine the arugula, spring mix, tomatoes, and radishes. Top with the Gorgonzola. Set aside.

COOK THE STEAKS: Heat a large skillet, preferably cast-iron, over medium-high heat. When the skillet is hot, remove the steaks from the marinade and add them to the pan. You may need to do this in batches, so as not to overcrowd the pan. Cook the steaks until seared on each side and cooked to preferred doneness, 3 to 4 minutes per side for medium, depending on thickness. Transfer the steaks to a cutting board and let rest for at least 5 minutes before slicing.

TO SERVE: Thinly slice the steaks against the grain. Place the sliced steak and its juices on top of the salad, drizzle with the desired amount of dressing.

FROM MY KITCHEN TO YOURS

The dressing keeps for 5 to 7 days in the refrigerator. It will thicken a bit in the fridge, so if you need to thin it out, add a splash of champagne vinegar or lemon juice.

SATISFYING SALADS AND BOWLS   31

Buffalo Caesar Bowls with Za'atar Chicken

MAKES 4 SERVINGS • TOTAL TIME: 25 MINUTES

When traveling during my first book tour, I would pop in and grab a salad from Sweetgreen any chance that I had! I love all of their salads, but since two of my favorite condiments are Buffalo sauce and Caesar dressing, their Buffalo Chicken Caesar was always my go-to order. I've eaten it more times than I can count! Here is my own riff on that beloved bowl. Salads can be a hard sell for picky eaters, but well-loved, familiar flavors like Buffalo sauce and Caesar makes this veggie-packed bowl a crowd-pleaser.

FOR THE QUICK-PICKLED VEGETABLES

½ cup julienned carrot (about 1 carrot)

¼ cup thinly sliced red onion

½ cup julienned celery (about 2 stalks)

2 tablespoons red wine vinegar

FOR THE CAESAR DRESSING

½ cup Homemade Mayo (page 251)

2 oil-packed anchovy fillets (or 1 teaspoon anchovy paste)

1 garlic clove, peeled

2 tablespoons freshly squeezed lemon juice (about 1 lemon)

1 tablespoon red wine vinegar

½ teaspoon Dijon mustard

½ teaspoon kosher salt

½ teaspoon freshly ground black pepper

FOR THE CHICKEN

1 pound boneless, skinless chicken breasts

2 tablespoons extra-virgin olive oil

2 teaspoons za'atar seasoning

1 teaspoon kosher salt

½ teaspoon freshly ground black pepper

QUICK-PICKLE THE VEGETABLES: In a large salad bowl, combine the carrot, onion, celery, and vinegar. Toss to coat. Set aside to "pickle" while you prepare the dressing.

MAKE THE CAESAR DRESSING: In a food processor or blender, combine the mayo, anchovies, garlic, lemon juice, vinegar, mustard, salt, and pepper. Blend until smooth. Set aside. (This keeps for 5 to 7 days in the refrigerator.)

MAKE THE CHICKEN: Place the chicken breasts on a cutting board and cover with parchment paper or plastic wrap. Using a meat mallet or the bottom of a heavy skillet, pound the chicken to a uniform ½-inch thickness. Pat dry with paper towels.

IN a large skillet, heat the olive oil over medium-high heat. Season the chicken breasts on both sides with the za'atar, salt, and pepper. Carefully place the chicken in the hot skillet and cook until golden brown on both sides and cooked through, 3 to 4 minutes per side. Transfer to a cutting board and let rest for 5 minutes before cutting.

MEANWHILE, MAKE THE SALAD: Add the romaine and kale to the pickled vegetables in the salad bowl. Next, add the radish, sesame seeds, and your desired amount of Caesar dressing. Toss until well combined and evenly coated with dressing.

TO SERVE: Cut the chicken into bite-size pieces and add to the salad, along with the blue cheese (if using). Toss to combine.

DRIZZLE with the Buffalo sauce immediately before serving.

FOR THE SALAD

3 cups finely chopped romaine lettuce

3 cups finely chopped stemmed and deribbed kale

1 red radish or watermelon radish, thinly sliced

2 tablespoons toasted sesame seeds

½ cup crumbled blue cheese (omit for dairy-free, paleo, and Whole30)

½ cup Buffalo sauce (I like The New Primal medium Buffalo sauce)

Chicken Paillard Salad with Thai Basil Green Goddess

GLUTEN-FREE
DAIRY-FREE
PALEO
WHOLE30
GRAIN-FREE

MAKES 4 SERVINGS • TOTAL TIME: 30 MINUTES

FOR THE THAI BASIL GREEN GODDESS DRESSING

1 cup Homemade Mayo (page 251)

4 oil-packed anchovy fillets (or 2 teaspoons anchovy paste)

2 garlic cloves, peeled

1 cup packed Thai basil leaves

½ cup roughly chopped green onion (about 2 green onions)

3 tablespoons freshly squeezed lemon juice (about 1½ lemons)

½ teaspoon kosher salt

¼ teaspoon freshly ground black pepper

FOR THE CHICKEN PAILLARDS

4 small boneless, skinless chicken breasts (about 8 ounces each)

1 teaspoon kosher salt

½ teaspoon freshly ground black pepper

¼ teaspoon cayenne pepper

2 tablespoons extra-virgin olive oil, plus more as needed

1 tablespoon freshly squeezed lemon juice (about ½ lemon)

FOR THE SALAD

2 heads butter lettuce, quartered through the stem

1 cup thinly sliced red radishes or watermelon radishes

½ cup roughly chopped Thai basil leaves

Thai basil is one of my absolute favorite herbs. Different from sweet basil, which is mostly used in Italian cooking, Thai basil has a slightly savory, sweet, and spicy-anise flavor to it. Using sweet basil is certainly okay in this recipe, but it just doesn't add that extra WOW factor like the Thai basil does. It's worth seeking out for this dish— trust me! It's a restaurant-worthy salad for sure!

MAKE THE GREEN GODDESS DRESSING: In a food processor or blender, combine the mayo, anchovies, garlic, Thai basil leaves, green onion, lemon, salt, and pepper and blend until smooth. Refrigerate until ready to use. (This keeps for 5 to 7 days in the refrigerator.)

MAKE THE CHICKEN PAILLARDS: With a sharp knife, trim the chicken breasts of any excess fat, then set them flat on a cutting board. Place one hand flat on top of a breast to hold it steady. With your other hand, hold the knife parallel to the cutting board and make a long, steady cut horizontally through the middle of the breast. Stop about ½ inch short of cutting all the way through. Open the chicken like a book. Place a piece of parchment paper or plastic wrap on top of the butterflied breast and use a meat mallet or the bottom of a heavy skillet to pound it to about a ¼-inch thickness. Pat dry with paper towels. Repeat with the remaining breasts.

SEASON both sides of the chicken with the salt, black pepper, and cayenne.

IN a large skillet, preferably cast-iron, heat the olive oil over medium-high heat. When the skillet is hot but not smoking, cook the chicken until golden brown on both sides and cooked through, 4 to 5 minutes per side. You'll likely have to do this in multiple batches, adding more oil to the pan if it becomes dry. Transfer the cooked chicken to a clean plate and drizzle with the lemon juice.

ASSEMBLE THE SALAD: In a large bowl, combine the butter lettuce, radishes, and Thai basil leaves. Drizzle and toss with your desired amount of the Green Goddess dressing.

TO SERVE: Divide the chicken and its juices among four plates and top with the dressed salad.

Salmon Fish Taco Bowls

MAKES 4 SERVINGS • TOTAL TIME: 25 MINUTES

FOR THE JALAPEÑO-CILANTRO DRESSING

¼ cup extra-virgin olive oil

½ cup loosely packed fresh cilantro leaves

¼ cup freshly squeezed lime juice (about 2 limes)

¼ cup roughly chopped seeded jalapeño (about 1 jalapeño)

2 teaspoons honey (omit for Whole30)

2 garlic cloves, peeled

½ teaspoon kosher salt

¼ teaspoon freshly ground black pepper

FOR THE SALMON

1½ teaspoons kosher salt

1 teaspoon chili powder

1 teaspoon ground cumin

½ teaspoon smoked paprika

½ teaspoon dried oregano

1 teaspoon garlic powder

4 center-cut salmon fillets (6 ounces each), skin removed

2 tablespoons extra-virgin olive oil

FOR THE SALAD

4 cups baby arugula

2 cups finely shredded red cabbage

1 cup halved and thinly sliced red onion

1 cup halved cherry tomatoes

1 cup cooked white rice (omit for grain-free, paleo, and Whole30)

1 avocado, thinly sliced

2 cups medium-diced mango

¼ cup fresh chopped cilantro, for garnish

Hot sauce, for serving

1 lime, cut into wedges, for serving

If you are a fish taco lover like me, this salmon fish taco bowl is going to rock your world. While the bowl is light and refreshing, it's still hearty enough—and it's certainly not lacking in the flavor department. The jalapeño-cilantro dressing might just be your new go-to favorite. Make a double batch and use it throughout the week!

MAKE THE JALAPEÑO-CILANTRO DRESSING: In a food processor or blender, combine the olive oil, cilantro, lime, jalapeño, honey (if using), garlic, salt, and pepper and blend until almost smooth. Set aside while you prepare the salmon.

COOK THE SALMON: In a small bowl, combine the salt, chili powder, cumin, smoked paprika, oregano, and garlic powder and stir to combine. Pat the salmon dry with paper towels. Evenly season the salmon fillets with the spice blend, rubbing the spices into all sides of the fish.

IN a nonstick skillet, heat the oil over medium-high heat. When the oil is hot but not smoking, place the salmon in the skillet and cook until golden brown and cooked through, 3 to 4 minutes per side. If the fillets are very thick, they may take an additional minute or two to cook through. Simply finish by turning the heat down to medium-low and cooking until the fish flakes easily when pressed with a fork. Transfer the cooked fish to a plate lined with paper towels.

ASSEMBLE THE SALADS: Evenly divide the arugula, cabbage, onion, tomatoes, rice (if using), avocado, and mango among four bowls. Top each bowl with a piece of salmon and drizzle with the desired amount of dressing. Garnish with fresh cilantro and serve with hot sauce and lime wedges.

Deconstructed Falafel Salad

MAKES 4 SERVINGS • TOTAL TIME: 40 MINUTES

FOR THE CRUNCHY CHICKPEAS

Two 15-ounce cans chickpeas, drained and rinsed

2 tablespoons extra-virgin olive oil

1 teaspoon ground cumin

1 teaspoon ground coriander

¼ teaspoon ground turmeric

1 teaspoon garlic powder

¼ teaspoon cayenne pepper

1 teaspoon kosher salt

½ teaspoon freshly ground black pepper

FOR THE TAHINI DRESSING

2 tablespoons tahini

1 teaspoon harissa

1 tablespoon freshly squeezed lemon juice (about ½ lemon)

1 garlic clove, minced

2 tablespoons extra-virgin olive oil

1 tablespoon honey

Pinch of kosher salt

FOR THE SALAD

8 cups deribbed and thinly sliced curly or lacinato kale (about 2 bunches)

½ cup roughly chopped fresh mint leaves

½ cup roughly chopped fresh dill fronds

¾ cup thinly sliced Persian (mini) cucumbers

¾ cup thinly sliced radishes

½ cup halved and thinly sliced red onion (see note)

1 avocado, thinly sliced

1 lemon, cut into wedges, for serving

Your favorite flavors from perfectly fried falafel come together in this fun salad! A delightful, slightly sweet tahini dressing tossed with greens and herbs, topped with fresh cucumber, onion, and, of course, spiced crunchy chickpeas! This salad is perfect for lunch or a quick, light weeknight meal.

PREHEAT the oven to 400°F. Line a sheet pan with parchment paper.

MAKE THE CHICKPEAS: Pour the chickpeas into a large bowl. Drizzle with the olive oil and season with the cumin, coriander, turmeric, garlic powder, cayenne, salt, and black pepper. Toss to coat the chickpeas evenly in the spice mixture.

TRANSFER the chickpeas to the prepared sheet pan, spread into an even layer, and bake until lightly browned and crisp, 25 to 30 minutes.

MEANWHILE, MAKE THE TAHINI DRESSING: In a small screw-top jar, combine the tahini, harissa, lemon juice, garlic, olive oil, honey, and salt. Cover and shake until well combined. If the dressing is too thick, add 1 to 2 tablespoons of warm water. Set aside.

MAKE THE SALAD: In a large bowl, combine the kale, mint, and dill. Pour your desired amount of dressing over the kale and toss continuously until the kale is well coated and slightly wilted, 2 to 3 minutes.

DIVIDE the salad mixture among four plates. Top each plate with the cucumbers, radishes, onion, avocado, and the chickpeas and serve with a lemon wedge.

FROM MY KITCHEN TO YOURS

If you don't love the taste of raw onions, you can take some of the bite out of them by soaking the sliced onions in warm water for 5 to 15 minutes. Then drain and add to the salad.

Chopped Chipotle Chicken Salad

MAKES 4 SERVINGS • TOTAL TIME: 30 MINUTES

FOR THE CHICKEN

1½ pounds boneless, skinless chicken thighs, trimmed of excess fat

2 tablespoons extra-virgin olive oil

2 tablespoons freshly squeezed lime juice (about 1 lime)

1 teaspoon dried oregano

1 teaspoon ground cumin

1 teaspoon smoked paprika

1 teaspoon kosher salt

½ teaspoon freshly ground black pepper

FOR THE CHIPOTLE DRESSING

1 cup Homemade Mayo (page 251)

3 garlic cloves, peeled

½ cup roughly chopped fresh cilantro leaves

1 teaspoon kosher salt

½ teaspoon freshly ground black pepper

¼ cup chipotle hot sauce (I use Siete Foods brand)

1 teaspoon chipotle chile powder

3 tablespoons freshly squeezed lime juice (about 1½ limes)

FOR THE SALAD

2 ears sweet corn, kernels removed (omit for paleo, Whole30, and grain-free)

1 tablespoon freshly squeezed lime juice (about ½ lime)

8 cups roughly chopped romaine lettuce

½ cup roasted, salted pumpkin seeds

1 cup cherry tomatoes, halved

½ cup halved and thinly sliced red onion

1 avocado, cut into ½-inch cubes

We eat this delicious chopped salad on repeat every summer. It never gets old! The star of the show is certainly the smoky, creamy chipotle dressing, but the layers of flavor added from the chicken, pumpkin seeds, and corn really shine, too!

MARINATE THE CHICKEN: In a large bowl, combine the chicken, olive oil, lime juice, oregano, cumin, smoked paprika, salt, and black pepper. Toss to coat the chicken evenly. Set aside to let the chicken marinate while you prepare the dressing. (The chicken can marinate up to 24 hours, covered in the fridge.)

MAKE THE CHIPOTLE DRESSING: In a food processor or blender, combine the mayo, garlic, cilantro, salt, black pepper, hot sauce, chipotle powder, and lime juice. Blend until smooth and set aside.

COOK THE CHICKEN: Heat a large skillet, preferably cast-iron, over medium-high heat. When hot, shake the excess marinade from the chicken, lay the chicken in the skillet, and cook until golden brown and cooked through, 4 to 5 minutes per side. Transfer the cooked chicken to a cutting board.

COOK THE CORN: Reduce the heat under the skillet to medium. Add the corn kernels (if using) to the skillet, then add the lime juice to deglaze the pan and pick up the flavor from the chicken. Cook, stirring occasionally, until the kernels are tender and the corn is lightly charred, 8 to 10 minutes. Remove from the heat and let cool.

MAKE THE SALAD: In a large bowl, combine the romaine, corn (if using), pumpkin seeds, tomatoes, and onion. Cut the chicken into bite-size pieces and add to the salad. Drizzle in your desired amount of dressing and toss until well coated. Add the avocado and gently toss to combine.

FROM MY KITCHEN TO YOURS

You'll likely have leftover dressing. It keeps well for 5 to 7 days in the fridge. Use it to dip fresh-cut veggies, drizzle it on any cooked protein, or even add it to sandwiches as a spread! It's such a great condiment to keep on hand for the week.

Harvest Salad with Miso Dressing

GLUTEN-FREE
DAIRY-FREE (IF MODIFIED)
VEGETARIAN

MAKES 4 SERVINGS • TOTAL TIME: 30 MINUTES

This seasonal salad is one of my favorites for the fall, but I certainly eat it year-round! I love the umami-spiked miso dressing alongside the warm, roasted sweet potatoes, tart, crisp apples, and creamy goat cheese. The recipe is meatless, but it's also great topped with shredded rotisserie chicken (for homemade, see Fauxtisserie Chicken, page 247) or sliced grilled steak!

FOR THE SWEET POTATOES

1½ pounds sweet potatoes, peeled, halved lengthwise, and thinly sliced

2 tablespoons extra-virgin olive oil

1 teaspoon kosher salt

½ teaspoon freshly ground black pepper

FOR THE DRESSING

¼ cup extra-virgin olive oil

1½ tablespoons gluten-free white miso (see note)

2 garlic cloves, grated

2 tablespoons apple cider vinegar

2 tablespoons freshly squeezed lemon juice (about 1 lemon)

Pinch of kosher salt

Pinch of freshly ground black pepper

FOR THE SALAD

5 cups curly or lacinato kale, deribbed and sliced into thin ribbons (about 1 bunch)

1 large Honeycrisp apple, cored, peeled, and cut into 1-inch pieces

2 cups cooked wild rice

½ cup crumbled goat cheese (omit for dairy-free)

½ cup lightly salted roasted pistachios

COOK THE SWEET POTATOES: Preheat the oven to 400°F. Line a sheet pan with parchment paper.

ARRANGE the sweet potatoes on the prepared sheet pan, drizzle with the olive oil, and season with the salt and pepper. Toss to coat well, then spread into an even layer. Roast until the sweet potatoes are tender and golden brown on the edges, 22 to 25 minutes.

MEANWHILE, MAKE THE DRESSING: In a large bowl, whisk the olive oil, miso, garlic, vinegar, lemon juice, salt, and pepper until well combined. Set aside.

ASSEMBLE THE SALAD: When there are about 10 minutes left on the sweet potato cook time, add the kale to the bowl with the dressing and toss until very well coated. Add the apple and toss. When the sweet potatoes are roasted and still warm, add to the salad along with the wild rice, goat cheese, and pistachios. Toss very gently once more.

DIVIDE the salad among four bowls and serve immediately.

FROM MY KITCHEN TO YOURS

Miso, a Japanese condiment, is a fermented paste made from beans and grains. Beans used can include soybeans, chickpeas, and adzuki beans, all of which are gluten-free. Grains used can include rice, millet, amaranth, and quinoa, which are gluten-free, or wheat, barley, and rye, which are not. To keep this dish gluten-free, you'll need to look closely for a brand of miso paste that is gluten-free. I like the Miso Master Organic Mellow White and Dom Miso that is marked as certified gluten-free.

Mediterranean Seared Tuna Salad

MAKES 4 SERVINGS • TOTAL TIME: 45 MINUTES

This seared tuna salad is light, fresh, savory, and colorful—how every salad should be! It was inspired by a salad served at Hillstone restaurants and is similar to a Niçoise but not as traditional. Like a Niçoise, the addition of potatoes helps absorb the bright and simple salad dressing and makes the salad more filling, leaving you nourished to take on the rest of your day.

FOR THE POTATOES

1 teaspoon kosher salt

1 pound yellow potatoes, peeled and cut into 2-inch chunks

FOR THE DRESSING

½ teaspoon Dijon mustard

½ teaspoon dried oregano

¼ cup extra-virgin olive oil

2 tablespoons red wine vinegar

2 tablespoons freshly squeezed lemon juice (about 1 lemon)

¼ teaspoon kosher salt

¼ teaspoon freshly ground black pepper

FOR THE TUNA

1 teaspoon paprika

1 teaspoon garlic powder

1 teaspoon dried oregano

1 teaspoon kosher salt

½ teaspoon freshly ground black pepper

4 bigeye or ahi tuna fillets (6 ounces each)

2 tablespoons avocado oil

FOR THE SALAD

8 cups coarsely chopped frisée lettuce

½ cup drained pitted kalamata olives

1 cup halved grape tomatoes

½ cup Marcona almonds

4 ounces goat cheese (omit for dairy-free, paleo, and Whole30)

COOK THE POTATOES: Bring a medium saucepan of salted water to a boil. Add the potatoes to the boiling water and cook until fork-tender, about 8 minutes. Drain and set aside to cool.

MEANWHILE, MAKE THE DRESSING: In a small bowl, combine the mustard, oregano, olive oil, vinegar, lemon juice, salt, and pepper and whisk until well combined. Set aside.

COOK THE TUNA: On a plate, combine the paprika, garlic powder, oregano, salt, and pepper. Mix until well combined. Press the tuna into the spice mixture to evenly coat on all sides.

IN a large nonstick skillet, heat the avocado oil over medium-high heat. Working in batches as needed, place the tuna in the skillet and sear it for 1 to 2 minutes per side, until a golden-brown crust has formed but the inside is still rare. Transfer the tuna to a cutting board and use a good, sharp knife to slice it into thin pieces.

ASSEMBLE THE SALAD: In a large bowl, combine the frisée, olives, tomatoes, almonds, and cooked potatoes. Top with the dressing and toss gently until well coated.

DIVIDE the salad among four plates and place the sliced tuna over the salad. Top with crumbled goat cheese, if using.

Vietnamese-Inspired "Shaking Beef" Salad

GLUTEN-FREE
DAIRY-FREE
PALEO
WHOLE30
GRAIN-FREE

MAKES 4 SERVINGS • TOTAL TIME: 25 MINUTES

Shaking Beef, known as bo luc lac or "dice" in Vietnamese, is a savory/sweet stir-fry that gets its English name from the constant shaking of the pan while browning the meat. I always enjoy eating this dish when dining out because the saucy steak bites are served over watercress for a peppery bite and finished with a tangy dressing for a dish packed with layers of flavor. With this dish in mind, I created my own rendition that I love making for small dinner parties and elevated date nights in. While full of impressive flavor, the entire dish comes together in under 30 minutes, giving your shallots just enough time to pickle to brighten up the whole dish. Enjoy as is, or spoon over rice.

FOR THE PICKLED SHALLOT VINAIGRETTE

¼ cup avocado oil

2 tablespoons red wine vinegar

1 teaspoon fish sauce

½ cup halved and thinly sliced shallot (about 1 large shallot)

FOR THE SALAD

8 cups watercress or baby arugula (8 ounces)

2 cups halved grape tomatoes

FOR THE SHAKING BEEF

2 garlic cloves, minced

1-inch piece fresh ginger, peeled and grated

2 tablespoons coconut aminos

1 teaspoon fish sauce

1 tablespoon rice vinegar

1 teaspoon Chinese five-spice powder

¼ teaspoon cayenne pepper

1½ pounds filet mignon, rib eye, or beef sirloin, cut into 1-inch cubes

1 teaspoon kosher salt

½ teaspoon freshly ground black pepper

1 tablespoon tapioca flour

2 tablespoons avocado oil

2 cups snow peas

MAKE THE PICKLED SHALLOT VINAIGRETTE: In a small bowl, whisk together the avocado oil, vinegar, and fish sauce until well combined. Add the shallot and set aside.

ASSEMBLE THE SALAD: Spread the watercress on a large platter and top with the tomatoes. Set aside.

COOK THE SHAKING BEEF: In a small bowl, combine the garlic, ginger, coconut aminos, fish sauce, vinegar, five-spice powder, and cayenne. Stir to combine and set aside.

SPRINKLE the steak pieces with the salt, black pepper, and tapioca flour. Toss until the steak is evenly coated.

IN a large nonstick skillet or wok, heat the avocado oil over medium-high heat. Add the steak in an even layer and cook until golden brown and crisp on all sides, about 2 minutes per side, 4 minutes total. Add the snow peas and coconut aminos mixture. Stir to combine, then cook stirring often, until the steak is cooked to your preference and the sauce has thickened, about 3 minutes for medium doneness.

TO SERVE: Drizzle half of the vinaigrette over the watercress and tomatoes. Gently toss to combine, adding more dressing to your liking. Using a slotted spoon, top the watercress with the steak and snow pea mixture. Serve immediately.

Sheet Pan Saffron Chicken Bowls

MAKES 4 SERVINGS • TOTAL TIME: 45 MINUTES

FOR THE MARINATED CHICKEN
1 teaspoon saffron threads
1 tablespoon warm water
¼ cup extra-virgin olive oil
⅓ cup plain Greek yogurt
¼ cup freshly squeezed lemon juice (about 2 lemons)
1 teaspoon ground turmeric
1 teaspoon onion powder
1½ teaspoons kosher salt
1 teaspoon freshly ground black pepper
2 pounds boneless, skinless chicken thighs, trimmed of excess fat and cut into 1-inch cubes

FOR THE ISRAELI SALAD
2 cups small-diced Persian (mini) cucumber (about 4 cucumbers)
1 cup seeded and small-diced Roma (plum) tomato (about 3 tomatoes)
1 cup minced red onion
¾ cup finely chopped curly parsley leaves
¼ cup extra-virgin olive oil
2 tablespoons freshly squeezed lemon juice (about 1 lemon)
½ teaspoon kosher salt, or more to taste
¼ teaspoon freshly ground black pepper, or more to taste

FOR THE CHICKEN AND VEGETABLES
2 Roma (plum) tomatoes, quartered
2 small white onions, peeled and cut into eigths
2 tablespoons extra-virgin olive oil

A friend introduced me to the delicious and very popular Persian dish joojeh kabob, which consists of tender chunks of saffron-infused chicken that is cooked on a skewer. With inspiration from the flavorful Persian kebab, I marinate tender chicken thighs in a delicious combination of saffron, Greek yogurt, and lemon juice. Then I cook it in the oven and serve it in bowls with a fresh Israeli salad, some rice, and a simple tahini drizzle. This bowl is delightful in every way.

PREHEAT the oven to 400°F. Line a large sheet pan with parchment paper.

MARINATE THE CHICKEN: In a large bowl, crush the saffron threads into little pieces using your fingers. Add the warm water, stir to combine, and set aside for 5 minutes, until fragrant. This will let the saffron threads bloom.

TO the bowl with the saffron, add the olive oil, yogurt, lemon juice, turmeric, onion powder, salt, and pepper. Stir to combine. Add the chicken, toss until well combined, and set aside to let marinate at room temperature for 10 minutes. (The chicken can marinate up to 24 hours covered in the fridge.)

MEANWHILE, MAKE THE ISRAELI SALAD: In a large bowl, combine the cucumber, tomato, red onion, and parsley. Drizzle with the olive oil and the lemon juice. Season with the salt and pepper. Set aside.

COOK THE CHICKEN AND VEGETABLES: Arrange the quartered tomatoes and onions on one side of the prepared sheet pan and toss with the olive oil. On the other half of the sheet pan, spread the marinated chicken in an even layer.

TRANSFER to the oven and roast until the chicken is cooked through, 23 to 25 minutes.

MEANWHILE, MAKE THE TAHINI DRIZZLE: In a small bowl, combine the tahini, lemon, garlic, warm water, and salt and whisk until well combined. If the sauce is thick or seizes up, add warm water in 1-tablespoon increments until it reaches your desired consistency.

TO SERVE: Evenly divide the rice among four bowls. Divide the chicken, charred tomatoes, and onions over the rice and top with your desired amount of Isreali salad and sprinkle with the pomegranate seeds. Drizzle with the tahini sauce.

FOR THE TAHINI DRIZZLE

½ cup tahini

2 tablespoons freshly squeezed lemon juice (about 1 lemon)

2 garlic cloves, minced

¼ cup warm water, plus more as needed

Kosher salt, to taste

FOR SERVING

2 cups cooked white rice

1 cup pomegranate seeds

savory soups

Creamy Cajun Chicken and Wild Rice Soup

GLUTEN-FREE
DAIRY-FREE

MAKES 4 SERVINGS • TOTAL TIME: 1 HOUR

This easy chicken and wild rice soup has a Cajun-spice twist to it that I just can't get enough of on a cold, rainy day. It's loaded with vegetables and wild rice and simmered in a delightful rich and creamy broth. If you love a good chicken soup and you love Cajun spices, this is a must-make!

2 tablespoons extra-virgin olive oil

1 cup small-diced yellow onion

1 cup small-diced green bell pepper

1 cup thinly sliced celery

2 garlic cloves, minced

1 teaspoon kosher salt, plus more to taste

½ teaspoon freshly ground black pepper, plus more to taste

1 teaspoon dried thyme

1 teaspoon paprika

1 teaspoon dried oregano

½ teaspoon dried rosemary

½ teaspoon cayenne pepper

8 cups (64 ounces) low-sodium chicken broth

2 bay leaves

1 cup uncooked wild rice

¾ cup dairy-free creamer or unsweetened full-fat coconut milk (sub heavy cream if not dairy-free)

2 tablespoons arrowroot flour

2 cups diced cooked chicken (I use rotisserie chicken, or see Fauxtisserie Chicken, page 247)

2 tablespoons freshly squeezed lemon juice (about 1 lemon)

2 tablespoons chopped fresh parsley, optional for garnish

IN a large pot or Dutch oven, heat the oil over medium heat. Add the onion, bell pepper, celery, and garlic and cook, stirring often, until the vegetables are tender, 5 to 7 minutes. Add the salt, black pepper, thyme, paprika, oregano, rosemary, and cayenne and cook, continuing to stir, until the spices are lightly toasted and fragrant, about 2 minutes.

ADD the chicken broth and bay leaves. Bring the soup to a boil. Reduce the heat to a simmer, add the rice, cover, and cook, stirring occasionally, until the rice is tender, about 45 minutes.

WHEN the rice is tender, in a small bowl, whisk together the dairy-free creamer (or coconut milk) and arrowroot flour until the flour has dissolved. While gently stirring the soup, slowly pour in the creamer mixture until well combined.

STIR in the cooked chicken and continue to cook the soup, uncovered and simmering, stirring often until thickened, 5 to 10 more minutes. Stir in the lemon juice. Taste and adjust the salt and pepper as desired. Discard the bay leaves.

TO SERVE: Ladle the soup into bowls and garnish with parsley, if desired.

Creamy Cauliflower Green Curry Soup

MAKES 4 SERVINGS • TOTAL TIME: 30 MINUTES

If you have been following me for a while, you already know my love for any soup is strong, but I have to say, creamy cauliflower soup is a favorite! It's light, healthy, and creamy without needing to include any dairy. With those characteristics in mind, I decided to amp up the flavor by simply including green curry paste and lemongrass. In a very short amount of time, you'll have the creaminess of a traditional cauliflower soup, but one packed with flavor and a brightness I cannot get enough of!

2 tablespoons extra-virgin olive oil, plus more for serving

½ cup thinly sliced shallots (about 2 shallots)

3 garlic cloves, minced

1 teaspoon kosher salt, plus more to taste

½ teaspoon freshly ground black pepper, plus more for serving

2 tablespoons green curry paste (I like Mae Ploy brand)

2 cups low-sodium vegetable broth

4 cups 2-inch cauliflower florets (stems included)

One 14-ounce can unsweetened full-fat coconut milk

1 large stalk lemongrass

1 teaspoon fish sauce (omit for vegetarian)

¼ cup chopped fresh cilantro, plus more to garnish

¼ cup chopped fresh Thai basil or regular basil

2 tablespoons freshly squeezed lemon juice (about 1 lemon)

IN a large pot or Dutch oven, heat the oil over medium heat. Add the shallots, garlic, salt, and pepper and cook, stirring often, until the shallot is tender, about 3 minutes. Add the green curry paste and stir until well combined. Sauté, stirring often, to bring out the flavors of the curry, about 1 minute. While stirring, slowly pour in 1 cup of the broth. Add the cauliflower, remaining 1 cup broth, and coconut milk.

USING the back of your knife, carefully pound the lemongrass on a cutting board, bruising it to release the flavor.

ADD the lemongrass, fish sauce (if using), cilantro, and basil to the soup. Bring to a boil, then reduce the heat to a simmer. Cover and cook until the cauliflower is fork-tender, about 15 minutes.

DISCARD the lemongrass. Transfer the soup to a high-powered blender and blend until very smooth.

RETURN the soup to the pot over low heat. Stir in the lemon juice. Taste and adjust the salt as desired. Ladle the soup into bowls to serve, drizzle with olive oil and freshly ground black pepper, and garnish with cilantro, if desired.

FROM MY KITCHEN TO YOURS

Have leftover green curry paste? Try making the Herby Green Curry Poached Halibut (page 175).

Easy Italian White Bean Soup

MAKES 4 SERVINGS • TOTAL TIME: 50 MINUTES

White beans are one of my absolute favorite pantry staples. They're mild in flavor, but when you use them in an herby, hearty soup like this they soak up all the fantastic flavors. It is one of those soups that's good for the soul and is a family favorite.

4 ounces bacon, pancetta, or ham (about 4 slices bacon), small-diced

1½ cups small-diced yellow onion (about 1 medium onion)

1 cup small-diced celery (about 2 stalks)

3 large garlic cloves, minced

½ teaspoon crushed red pepper flakes

¼ cup dry white wine

Two 15-ounce cans no-salt-added cannellini beans, drained and rinsed

4 cups (32 ounces) low-sodium vegetable or chicken broth

1 Parmesan cheese rind (omit for dairy-free)

1 teaspoon dried rosemary

½ teaspoon dried oregano

1 bay leaf

Grated zest of ½ lemon

1 teaspoon kosher salt, plus more to taste

½ teaspoon freshly ground black pepper, plus more to taste

3 cups baby spinach

2 tablespoons freshly squeezed lemon juice (about 1 lemon)

2 tablespoons chopped fresh parsley, for serving

Extra-virgin olive oil, for serving

¼ cup freshly grated Parmesan cheese, for serving (omit for dairy-free)

HEAT a Dutch oven or large soup pot over medium heat. Add the bacon and cook, stirring often, until the bacon is almost cooked and the fat has begun to render, 3 to 4 minutes.

ADD the onion, celery, garlic, pepper flakes, and cook, stirring, until the vegetables are tender, about 5 minutes. Add the wine and continue to cook, stirring and scraping up any of the browned bits on the bottom, until the wine has reduced by half, about 2 minutes.

ADD the beans, broth, Parmesan rind (if using), rosemary, oregano, bay leaf, lemon zest, salt, and pepper and bring the soup to a boil. Reduce the heat to a light simmer, cover, and cook for about 25 minutes, stirring occasionally.

DISCARD the bay leaf and Parmesan rind. Stir in the spinach and lemon juice. Taste and add more salt and pepper if desired. Continue to cook, uncovered and simmering, about 5 more minutes.

SERVE in bowls and top with the parsley, a drizzle of olive oil, and freshly grated Parmesan (if using).

French Onion Beef Stew

MAKES 4 SERVINGS • TOTAL TIME: 2 HOURS 5 MINUTES

Growing up, I used to love how my mom would use a packet of French onion soup mix to make all sorts of recipes: dips, casseroles, pot roasts, and more. Here I've taken that packet of seasoning as inspiration to make a delicious beef stew. It's a total crowd-pleaser at our family dinner table! While the cook time is long, it is mostly hands-off, and I find there's something about a stew simmering on the stove that brings an atmosphere of comfort to your kitchen, whether it's a weekend or a weeknight.

2 pounds beef round roast, cut into 2-inch cubes

2 teaspoons kosher salt, plus more to taste

½ teaspoon freshly ground black pepper, plus more to taste

1 tablespoon arrowroot flour

3 tablespoons extra-virgin olive oil

2 cups halved and thinly sliced yellow onions (about 2 small onions)

2 garlic cloves, thinly sliced

½ cup red wine

1 teaspoon Dijon mustard

2 bay leaves

2 teaspoons dried parsley

4 teaspoons onion powder

1 teaspoon garlic powder

1 teaspoon paprika

4 small yellow potatoes, cut into 2-inch cubes (about 2½ cups)

2 cups low-sodium beef broth

2 tablespoons brine from a jar of pepperoncini

5 fresh thyme sprigs, tied into a bundle with kitchen twine, plus more for serving

2 tablespoons chopped fresh parsley, optional for serving

IN a large bowl, sprinkle the meat with the salt, pepper, and arrowroot flour. Toss to coat the meat evenly.

IN a large pot or Dutch oven, heat the oil over medium-high heat. Add the beef in a single layer and brown until golden brown on all sides, about 2 minutes per side. You will likely need to do this in two or three batches to ensure you do not overcrowd the pot and the beef gets a nice sear. Transfer the browned meat to a plate and set aside.

REDUCE the heat to medium and add the onions and garlic. Cook, stirring often, for 3 minutes. Add the wine and mustard and use the edge of a wooden spoon to scrape up the browned bits from the bottom of the pan. Continue to cook, stirring, until the onions are tender and the wine has reduced by half, 2 to 3 minutes. Stir in the bay leaves, parsley, onion powder, garlic powder, and paprika.

RETURN the beef and its juices to the pot and add the potatoes. Toss until well combined. Add the beef broth, pepperoncini brine, and thyme bundle and increase the heat to bring the stew to a boil. Reduce the heat to a low simmer, cover, and cook until the meat is very tender, about 1 hour 15 minutes.

UNCOVER, stir, and continue to cook for about 15 more minutes, until the stew is thickened to your liking. Taste the broth and add more salt and pepper to taste. Discard the bay leaves and thyme bundle.

SERVE in bowls topped with fresh thyme leaves and parsley, if desired.

GoGo's Healing Creamy Mushroom Soup

MAKES 4 SERVINGS • TOTAL TIME: 45 MINUTES

GLUTEN-FREE
DAIRY-FREE
PALEO
WHOLE30
GRAIN-FREE
VEGETARIAN

My mother-in-law, GoGo, makes soup like it's her job! I don't think there has been a time that I have walked through her kitchen without a pot of soup on the stovetop simmering away. Each recipe she makes is as delightful as the one before. A breast cancer survivor, she was recommended this particular soup by a doctor as she was battling the disease. Mushrooms are known for their lengthy list of health benefits, including supporting the immune system, so she ate this soup frequently during her treatment. Aside from being a healthy bowl of soup packed with antioxidant-heavy mushrooms, it's a delicious and comforting recipe that our family has fallen in love with.

2 tablespoons extra-virgin olive oil, plus more for serving

4 garlic cloves, minced

2 cups medium-diced yellow onion (about 1 large onion)

1 cup medium-diced celery (about 2 stalks), leaves included

1 teaspoon kosher salt

½ teaspoon freshly ground black pepper

6 cups (48 ounces) low-sodium vegetable or chicken broth

16 ounces white mushrooms, quartered

16 ounces baby bella mushrooms, quartered

4 cups coarsely chopped romaine lettuce (about 1 large head)

2 tablespoons fresh thyme leaves, for serving

Flaky salt, optional for serving

IN a large pot or Dutch oven, heat the oil over medium heat. Add the garlic, onion, celery, salt, and pepper and cook, stirring often, until the veggies are tender, 5 to 7 minutes. Add the broth, mushrooms, and romaine and stir to combine. Bring the soup to a simmer, cover, and cook for 15 minutes.

UNCOVER and continue to cook until the broth reduces by one-quarter, 15 to 20 more minutes.

WORKING carefully in two or three batches, transfer the soup to a high-powered blender and blend until silky smooth.

SERVE in bowls garnished with a drizzle of olive oil, a sprinkle of fresh thyme leaves, and a pinch of flaky salt, if desired.

Easy Greek-Inspired Lemon Chicken Soup

MAKES 4 SERVINGS • TOTAL TIME: 30 MINUTES

I love going to my favorite local Greek restaurant, Platia Greek Kouzina in Frisco, Texas, and enjoying a hot cup of avgolemono soup. It's a silky, rich, fragrant chicken soup, prepared Greek-style with avgolemono sauce (a lemon-egg sauce). This certainly isn't avgolemono, but it's definitely inspired by it. Rather than making the broth silky by adding the lemon-egg sauce, I used Israeli couscous in this Greek-inspired soup, which contributes to the creaminess of the soup. The hearty chicken paired with the fresh herbs and bright lemon flavor makes this a definite go-to chicken soup for my family!

2 tablespoons extra-virgin olive oil

¾ cup small-diced carrot (about 1 medium carrot)

¾ cup small-diced celery (about 2 stalks)

¾ cup small-diced yellow onion (about ¾ medium onion)

2 garlic cloves, minced

1 teaspoon kosher salt, plus more to taste

½ teaspoon freshly ground black pepper

½ teaspoon paprika

¼ teaspoon cayenne pepper, optional

4 cups (32 ounces) low-sodium chicken broth

2 cups medium-diced cooked chicken (I use a rotisserie chicken, or see Fauxtisserie Chicken, page 247)

¼ cup freshly squeezed lemon juice (about 2 lemons)

1 bay leaf

1 cup Israeli or pearl couscous

1 teaspoon grated lemon zest

2 tablespoons chopped fresh parsley leaves

2 tablespoons chopped fresh oregano

2 tablespoons chopped fresh dill, plus more for serving

IN a large pot or Dutch oven, heat the oil over medium heat. When the oil is hot, add the carrot, celery, onion, garlic, salt, black pepper, paprika, and cayenne (if using). Cook, stirring, until the vegetables are tender, 5 to 7 minutes.

INCREASE the heat to medium-high and add the broth, chicken, lemon juice, and bay leaf. Bring to a boil, then reduce the heat to a light simmer and add the couscous, lemon zest, parsley, and oregano. Cook, uncovered and stirring occasionally, until the couscous is tender, about 10 minutes. Stir in the dill. Taste and add more salt, if desired. Discard the bay leaf.

LADLE the soup into bowls to serve and garnish with more dill.

Broccoli and Cheddar Soup

MAKES 4 SERVINGS • TOTAL TIME: 30 MINUTES

GLUTEN-FREE
GRAIN-FREE
DAIRY-FREE (IF MODIFIED)
VEGETARIAN

Is there anything better than a steaming hot bowl of creamy broccoli and cheddar soup? Such a classic! Here I've taken the classic broccoli and cheddar soup and made it more nutritious. The base of this soup is filled with cauliflower and sweet potato, resulting in a creamy, nutrient-dense soup that still tastes like the original one you love and enjoy.

2 tablespoons extra-virgin olive oil

1 cup small-diced yellow onion

4 garlic cloves, peeled

1½ cups peeled and cubed (1-inch) sweet potato (about 1 medium sweet potato)

8 cups cauliflower florets (about 2 small heads)

4 cups (32 ounces) low-sodium vegetable or chicken broth

2 teaspoons kosher salt, plus more to taste

½ teaspoon freshly ground black pepper, plus more to taste

2 teaspoons garlic powder

2 teaspoons onion powder

1 teaspoon paprika

¼ teaspoon cayenne pepper

2 cups freshly shredded mild cheddar cheese (I like Tillamook; sub dairy-free shredded cheese for dairy-free)

¾ cup dairy-free creamer (sub heavy cream or whole milk if not dairy-free)

4 cups coarsely chopped broccoli (about 1 head)

IN a large pot or Dutch oven, heat the oil over medium heat. Add the onion and garlic and cook, stirring often, until the onion is tender, about 3 minutes. Add the sweet potato, cauliflower, broth, salt, pepper, garlic powder, onion powder, paprika, and cayenne and bring the soup to a boil. Reduce the heat to a simmer, cover, and cook until the cauliflower is fork-tender, 10 to 15 minutes.

WORKING carefully in two or three batches, transfer the soup to a high-powered blender and blend until very smooth. With the last batch, add the cheddar and creamer and blend once more until silky smooth.

RETURN the soup to the pot, taste the soup base, and add salt and pepper to taste. Add the broccoli, bring the soup to a simmer, and cook, uncovered, until the broccoli is tender, about 5 minutes.

Lamb and Potato Samosa–Inspired Stew with Mint Chutney Drizzle

MAKES 6 SERVINGS • TOTAL TIME: 35 MINUTES

FOR THE LAMB AND POTATO STEW

2 tablespoons extra-virgin olive oil

2 cups minced yellow onion (about 2 medium onions)

2 garlic cloves, minced

1-inch knob fresh ginger, peeled and finely grated

1½ teaspoons kosher salt

½ teaspoon freshly ground black pepper

2 pounds ground lamb

1 teaspoon ground cumin

1 teaspoon ground coriander

1 teaspoon garam masala

½ teaspoon cayenne pepper

½ teaspoon ground turmeric

2 tablespoons tomato paste

4 cups (32 ounces) low-sodium beef broth

4 cups peeled and cubed (½-inch) russet potatoes (about 2 potatoes)

FOR THE MINT CHUTNEY DRIZZLE

1 cup loosely packed fresh mint leaves

1 cup loosely packed fresh cilantro

3 tablespoons roughly chopped seeded jalapeño

2 tablespoons freshly squeezed lemon juice (about 1 lemon)

⅓ cup extra-virgin olive oil

Pinch of kosher salt

Pinch of freshly ground black pepper

TO FINISH

1½ cups frozen peas

1 tablespoon freshly squeezed lemon juice (about ½ lemon)

When dining out at Indian restaurants, our family always orders samosas to start: A fried or baked pastry stuffed with beautifully seasoned potatoes, vegetables, and/or meat—what better way to start a meal? Samosas are absolutely delightful, and dipping them in a lovely chutney just sets the experience over the top. I made this samosa-inspired stew for the first time because I happened to have some lamb in the freezer and fresh herbs on hand and, when you really break down this recipe, most of the ingredients are pantry staples! It's certainly far from a real samosa, but I love how the similar flavors come together for a hearty stew. Topped with a drizzle of the spicy mint chutney, this stew is certain to make your taste buds sing!

MAKE THE LAMB AND POTATO STEW: In a large pot or Dutch oven, heat the oil over medium-high heat. Add the onion, garlic, ginger, salt, and pepper and cook, stirring, until the onion is tender, 5 to 7 minutes.

ADD the ground lamb and cook, breaking up the meat with a wooden spoon, until browned and cooked through, 5 to 7 minutes. Drain the excess fat and return the meat to the pot. Add the cumin, coriander, garam masala, cayenne, and turmeric and cook, stirring until the spices are fragrant, about 2 minutes.

STIR in the tomato paste. Add the beef broth and potatoes and bring the soup to a boil. Reduce the heat to a simmer and cook, uncovered, until the potatoes are tender, about 8 minutes.

MEANWHILE, MAKE THE DRIZZLE: In a food processor or blender, combine the mint, cilantro, jalapeño, lemon juice, olive oil, salt, and pepper. Blend until smooth.

TO FINISH THE STEW: Stir the peas and lemon juice into the stew. Cook until the peas are tender, about 3 minutes.

LADLE the soup into bowls and top with a dollop of the drizzle.

Spicy Miso Ramen with Pork

GLUTEN-FREE
DAIRY-FREE

MAKES 4 SERVINGS • TOTAL TIME: 35 MINUTES

Craving a comforting bowl of ramen noodles at home but want to fancy up the usual package of ramen? Well, this spicy miso ramen is the way to do it! It's a quick and easy version to make—thanks to a carton of broth—but with all the added spices, pork, and miso, the finished product is beyond flavorful and absolutely delightful.

1 pound ground pork

4 garlic cloves, very thinly sliced

½ cup finely chopped shallots (about 2 shallots)

1 cup sliced shiitake mushrooms

1 tablespoon toasted sesame oil

1 teaspoon crushed red pepper flakes

1 teaspoon cayenne pepper

1 teaspoon Sichuan peppercorns, crushed (I place in a bag and crush using the back of a spoon)

¼ cup gluten-free white miso (see note on page 43)

4 cups (32 ounces) low-sodium beef broth

1 cup unsweetened full-fat coconut milk

2 tablespoons coconut aminos

One 14-ounce can bamboo shoots, drained and rinsed

1 cup thinly sliced green onions (about 4 green onions)

2 tablespoons freshly squeezed lime juice (about 1 lime)

Kosher salt and freshly ground black pepper, to taste

4 large eggs

5 ounces gluten-free ramen noodles (I use Lotus Foods brown rice ramen)

½ cup thinly sliced nori (about 4 sheets), for garnish

Toasted sesame seeds, for garnish

HEAT a large pot or Dutch oven over medium-high heat. Add the ground pork and cook, breaking it up with a wooden spoon, until browned and cooked through (no longer pink), 5 to 7 minutes. Using a slotted spoon, transfer the pork to a plate and set aside, leaving the pork fat in the pot.

REDUCE the heat to medium and add the garlic, shallots, and mushrooms. Cook, stirring, until the shallots and mushrooms are tender, 3 to 4 minutes. Add the sesame oil, pepper flakes, cayenne, and Sichuan peppercorns and cook, stirring often, until the spices are lightly toasted and fragrant, about 1 minute.

ADD the miso and stir until well combined. While stirring, gradually pour in 1 cup of the broth and stir until the miso is mixed in well. Pour in the remaining 3 cups broth, the coconut milk, and coconut aminos. Return the cooked pork and any of its juices to the pot. Add the bamboo shoots, green onions, and lime juice. Taste and season with salt and black pepper to taste. Bring the broth to a boil, then reduce the heat to a simmer, cover, and continue to cook while you prepare the eggs and noodles.

SET up a bowl of ice and water and set aside. Bring a medium saucepan of water to a boil. Using a slotted spoon, carefully lower the eggs into the boiling water and cook for 6½ minutes. With the slotted spoon, transfer the eggs to the ice water to cool.

ADD the ramen noodles to the boiling water and cook according to the package directions.

TO SERVE: Divide the cooked ramen noodles among four bowls. Ladle the soup over the noodles. Peel the soft-boiled eggs, halve them, and place them in the ramen. Garnish with the nori strips and sesame seeds.

FROM MY KITCHEN TO YOURS

Have leftover miso paste? Try making the Harvest Salad with Miso Dressing (page 43) or the Miso-Broiled Halibut (page 189).

Zuppa Toscana

MAKES 4 SERVINGS • TOTAL TIME: 30 MINUTES

Here is a popular recipe from my blog that was inspired by another childhood favorite of mine: Olive Garden's Zuppa Toscana. The endless breadsticks unfortunately do not come with it but I promise you will be comforted by the delicious and nostalgic flavor of this soup. If you are not familiar with it, it is one you will not want to skip! It has a rich, creamy broth, without any dairy. The chunky potato and spicy Italian sausage are full of flavor and will leave those who usually do not see soup as a meal nourished and satisfied.

2 slices bacon, roughly chopped

1 cup minced yellow onion (about ½ medium onion)

4 garlic cloves, minced

½ teaspoon kosher salt

½ teaspoon freshly ground black pepper

1 pound hot Italian pork sausage (if you buy it in links, remove from the casings)

2 tablespoons arrowroot flour

4 cups (32 ounces) low-sodium chicken broth

1 teaspoon Italian seasoning

4 cups chopped deribbed lacinato kale (about 1 bunch)

2 cups peeled and cubed (½-inch) russet potatoes (about 1 large potato)

1 cup dairy-free creamer (sub heavy cream if not dairy-free)

1 tablespoon nutritional yeast (sub ¼ cup grated Parmesan cheese if not dairy-free)

2 tablespoons freshly squeezed lemon juice (about 1 lemon)

2 tablespoons chopped fresh parsley, optional for garnish

HEAT a large pot or Dutch oven over medium heat. Add the bacon and cook, stirring occasionally, until just crispy, 4 to 6 minutes. Using a slotted spoon, transfer the cooked bacon to a plate lined with paper towels and set aside, reserving the bacon fat in the pot.

ADD the onion, garlic, salt, pepper, and sausage to the pot and cook, breaking up the meat with a wooden spoon, until cooked through and no longer pink, 4 to 5 minutes.

ADD the arrowroot flour and stir until well incorporated into the meat mixture. While stirring, slowly pour in the chicken broth. Bring the soup to a boil, reduce the heat to a simmer, and add the Italian seasoning, kale, and potatoes. Cover and cook until the potatoes are tender, 10 to 15 minutes.

UNCOVER and stir in the creamer and nutritional yeast. Simmer for 5 minutes to let the flavors meld with the creamer. Stir in the lemon juice.

SERVE in bowls topped with the cooked bacon bits and garnish with parsley, if desired.

pasta, pasta, pasta

Mom's Anchovy Pasta

MAKES 4 SERVINGS • TOTAL TIME: 20 MINUTES

2 tablespoons extra-virgin olive oil

6 oil-packed anchovy fillets (or 4 teaspoons anchovy paste)

¼ cup minced shallot (about 1 large shallot)

4 garlic cloves, very thinly sliced

1 teaspoon crushed red pepper flakes, plus more for serving

1 cup dry white wine

One 14-ounce can cherry tomatoes (see note), undrained

1 tablespoon chopped fresh flat-leaf parsley, plus more for serving

1 teaspoon kosher salt, plus more to taste

½ teaspoon freshly ground black pepper

8 ounces bucatini pasta (sub gluten-free spaghetti for gluten-free)

Grated Parmesan cheese, optional for serving (omit for dairy-free)

FROM MY KITCHEN TO YOURS

Canned cherry tomatoes can be tricky to find, but I very strongly recommend that you track them down for this recipe. I typically stock up on canned cherry tomatoes at my local Italian grocery store. If you simply can't find them, you can use one 28-ounce can whole peeled San Marzano tomatoes. Drain and cut them into medium dice. You'll have a chunkier pasta sauce—but it'll still be delicious.

I'm sure many of you are going to want to turn the page and "kindly pass" on a recipe with anchovy in the name, but please don't! First off, if you think you don't like anchovies, I guarantee you've eaten plenty of them in restaurants. They're a secret weapon in the kitchen and add a salty, umami flavor to dishes. This is a dish that my mom loved to make on busy weeknights when she didn't have any fresh food in the fridge, as it uses pantry staples and is easy to prepare. Best of all, it's simply delicious and reminds me of my bucatini- and anchovy-loving mom with every bite.

BRING a large pot of water to a boil.

MEANWHILE, in a large deep skillet, heat the oil over medium heat. Add the anchovies, shallot, and garlic and cook, stirring and breaking up the anchovies with a wooden spoon, until the anchovies have turned into a paste and the shallot is tender, 3 to 4 minutes. Add the pepper flakes and cook, stirring often, for 1 minute.

POUR in the wine and cook, stirring often, until the wine has reduced by half, 2 to 3 minutes. Add the tomatoes, parsley, salt, and black pepper and stir to combine. Bring the sauce to a simmer, cover, and cook until the tomatoes have softened, about 5 minutes. Use the back of a wooden spoon to pop open the softened tomatoes and release their juices. Reduce the heat to low, cover, and keep warm while you prepare the pasta.

ADD the pasta and a heavy pinch of salt (about 1 tablespoon) to the boiling water and cook according to the package directions.

RESERVE about 1 cup of the starchy pasta water and set aside. Drain the pasta and transfer to the skillet with the sauce. Toss thoroughly for 2 to 3 minutes to allow the sauce to absorb into and coat the bucatini. If the pasta is sticking together or a bit dry, slowly add small increments of the pasta water, about ¼ cup at a time (you likely won't need the entire cup). Taste the pasta and add more salt, if desired.

SERVE the pasta in bowls and garnish with grated Parmesan (if using), parsley, and pepper flakes.

One-Pot Beef Stroganoff

|| GLUTEN-FREE (IF MODIFIED)

MAKES 4 SERVINGS • TOTAL TIME: 25 MINUTES

Beef stroganoff made in one pot in less than 30 minutes? Yes, please! If you were like me and grew up on the boxed version from Hamburger Helper, this will bring you right back to your childhood. You get all the nostalgia in the same amount of time as the original, but with a much more elevated result. Perfect for a weeknight or a lazy Sunday, this is sure to be a family favorite.

2 tablespoons extra-virgin olive oil

1 cup minced yellow onion (about ½ medium onion)

1 pound ground beef

1 teaspoon kosher salt, plus more to taste

½ teaspoon garlic powder

½ teaspoon onion powder

½ teaspoon paprika

½ teaspoon freshly ground black pepper

2 teaspoons Dijon mustard

1 cup thinly sliced cremini mushrooms

4 cups wide egg noodles (sub Jovial Brown Rice Egg Tagliatelle for gluten-free)

4 cups (32 ounces) low-sodium beef broth

2 tablespoons white wine vinegar

8 ounces light sour cream

1 teaspoon fresh thyme leaves, for serving

1 tablespoon chopped fresh parsley leaves, optional for serving

IN a large skillet, heat the oil over medium-high heat. Add the onion and cook, stirring often, until the onion begins to brown, 2 to 3 minutes. Add the ground beef and season with the salt, garlic powder, onion powder, paprika, and pepper. Cook, breaking up the meat with a wooden spoon, until browned and no longer pink, 5 to 7 minutes. If there is too much grease, drain it off, reserving about 2 tablespoons in the pan to sauté the mushrooms in.

ADD the mustard and mushrooms to the pan and stir until well combined. Sauté, stirring often, until the mushrooms have soaked up some of the fat and are softened, 3 to 4 minutes.

ADD the noodles, broth, and vinegar, bring to a boil, and cook, stirring often, until the noodles are tender and most of the liquid has been absorbed, about 12 minutes.

REMOVE the skillet from the heat and stir in the sour cream and thyme. Taste and add more salt, if desired. Garnish with parsley, if using.

Orecchiette alla Vodka

MAKES 6 SERVINGS • TOTAL TIME: 30 MINUTES

You've likely had vodka sauce over penne—the traditional way to enjoy the dish—but I just love serving vodka sauce tossed with orecchiette pasta. The little cups encase the creamy tomato sauce in the most magnificent way! But feel free to use whatever pasta your heart desires. And if you're wondering if vodka is a necessary element in this recipe, the answer is yes! The vodka absolutely alters the flavor of the sauce by adding a touch of sharpness and heat that help balance out the sweetness from the tomatoes and cream.

4 ounces diced pancetta

¾ cup chopped shallots (about 2 shallots)

3 garlic cloves, minced

½ teaspoon crushed red pepper flakes

1 teaspoon kosher salt, plus more to taste

½ teaspoon freshly ground black pepper

¼ cup vodka

One 28-ounce can San Marzano tomatoes, crushed by hand (see note)

1 pound orecchiette (sub gluten-free pasta for gluten-free)

½ cup heavy cream

½ cup freshly grated Parmesan cheese, plus more for serving

2 tablespoons thinly sliced fresh basil leaves, optional for serving

PAIRING SUGGESTION: **Little Gem Salad with Lemon Dressing (page 204)**

BRING a large pot of water to a boil.

MEANWHILE, heat a large deep skillet over medium heat. Add the pancetta and cook, stirring, until golden brown and crisp, 5 to 7 minutes. Add the shallots, garlic, pepper flakes, salt, and the black pepper and cook, stirring often, until the shallots are tender, 3 to 4 minutes. Add the vodka and cook, stirring often, until the vodka has reduced by half, about 2 minutes. Pour in the crushed tomatoes and stir to combine. Bring the sauce to a simmer and cook, stirring often, for 5 minutes or so while the pasta starts cooking.

MEANWHILE, add plenty of salt (about 1 tablespoon) and the pasta to the boiling water and cook until al dente according to the package directions.

STIR the heavy cream into the sauce, bring to a light simmer, and cook, stirring often, while the pasta finishes cooking.

DRAIN the pasta, transfer it to the sauce, and add the Parmesan. Toss the pasta with the sauce until very well coated, about 2 minutes, then remove from the heat. Taste and add more salt, if desired.

SERVE immediately topped with more Parmesan. If desired, garnish with the basil.

FROM MY KITCHEN TO YOURS

Pour the can of tomatoes, undrained, into a large bowl. Using your hands, crush the tomatoes until they reach a pulp-like consistency.

Spicy Shrimp Pasta with Tarragon and Basil

|| GLUTEN-FREE (IF MODIFIED)

MAKES 4 SERVINGS • TOTAL TIME: 25 MINUTES

If you ever find yourself in Dallas, Texas, I cannot recommend enough treating yourself to a lovely dinner at The Charles restaurant. It is one of Clayton's and my favorite date-night dinner spots and we always have a good time! While I love all of their pasta dishes, their Spicy Creste di Gallo is an absolute showstopper—a combination of rock shrimp, tarragon, basil, and lemon tossed with a handmade spicy pasta. Inspired by their dish, I've made my own at-home variation and it's simply delicious!

Kosher salt, to taste

8 ounces creste di gallo, trumpet, or casarecce pasta (sub gluten-free pasta for gluten-free)

2 tablespoons unsalted butter

1 tablespoon extra-virgin olive oil

¼ cup thinly sliced shallot (about 1 large shallot)

4 garlic cloves, thinly sliced

1 teaspoon crushed red pepper flakes

1 pound peeled, deveined, and tail-off shrimp (31/40 count), cut into ¼-inch pieces

Grated zest of ½ lemon

2 tablespoons finely chopped fresh tarragon leaves

2 tablespoons finely chopped fresh basil

1 cup freshly grated Pecorino-Romano cheese, plus more for serving

2 tablespoons freshly squeezed lemon juice (about 1 lemon)

Freshly ground black pepper, to taste

BRING a large pot of water to a boil. Add plenty of salt (I use 1 tablespoon) and the pasta and cook until al dente, according to the package directions.

MEANWHILE, in a large deep skillet, melt the butter over medium heat and add the oil. Add the shallot, garlic, and pepper flakes and cook, stirring often, until the shallot is just tender, about 2 minutes. Add the shrimp, lemon zest, tarragon, and basil and cook, stirring often, until the shrimp is opaque and cooked through, about 3 minutes. Using a slotted spoon, transfer the cooked shrimp to a plate and set aside so as to not overcook it.

RESERVE 1 cup of the pasta water and drain the pasta. In the same pan that you cooked the shrimp in, over medium heat, add the pasta, Pecorino-Romano cheese, and lemon juice and toss to combine. Slowly stir in ½ cup of the reserved pasta water. Toss again until well coated, 2 to 3 minutes. If the pasta is sticking together or a bit dry, slowly add small increments of more pasta water, about ¼ cup at a time (you likely won't need the entire cup).

RETURN the shrimp to the pasta and toss once more to combine. Add salt and pepper to taste. Serve with additional grated Pecorino-Romano.

The Best Bolognese

MAKES 8 TO 10 SERVINGS • TOTAL TIME: 5 HOURS (MOSTLY UNATTENDED)

4 ounces diced pancetta

6 oil-packed anchovy fillets (or 3 teaspoons anchovy paste)

2 cups minced yellow onion (about 1 large onion)

1 cup minced peeled carrot (about 1 large carrot)

¾ cup minced celery (about 1 large stalk)

4 garlic cloves, minced

1½ pounds ground beef

1 pound ground pork

1 pound ground veal

2 teaspoons kosher salt, plus more to taste

1 teaspoon freshly ground black pepper, plus more to taste

½ cup dry white wine

One 28-ounce can San Marzano tomatoes, crushed by hand (see note, page 78)

One 15-ounce can tomato sauce

One 6-ounce can tomato paste

1 Parmesan cheese rind (omit for dairy-free)

2 bay leaves

10 fresh thyme sprigs, tied into a bundle with kitchen twine

1 cup whole milk (sub dairy-free creamer if dairy-free)

FOR SERVING

Pasta of choice, cooked al dente according to package directions and 1 cup of pasta water reserved

Freshly grated Parmesan cheese (omit for dairy-free)

Fresh thyme leaves

PAIRING SUGGESTION: Sileo Celery Salad with Charcuterie (page 16)

This is seriously the best Bolognese sauce! While there are many different interpretations of Bolognese around the world, this is how I learned to make it in my Italian family. The smell takes me straight back to my childhood, and it makes me so happy to let a big batch simmer on the stovetop all day long. It's the dinner that is most requested for birthdays in my family, and one that I know my children will continue to make and enjoy forever.

HEAT a large pot or Dutch oven over medium-high heat. Add the pancetta and cook, stirring occasionally, until the fat is rendered and the pancetta is just crisp, 4 to 5 minutes.

ADD the anchovies, onion, carrot, celery, and garlic. Cook, stirring often and mashing up the anchovies so that they break up into a paste, until the veggies are tender, 5 to 7 minutes.

ADD the ground beef, pork, veal, salt, and pepper and cook, breaking up the meat with a wooden spoon, until the meat is just cooked through, 8 to 10 minutes. Drain off the excess fat if necessary (I like to leave 2 to 3 tablespoons in there for flavor!).

ADD the wine and cook, stirring, until the wine is reduced by half, about 3 minutes. Add the tomatoes, tomato sauce, and tomato paste and stir until well combined. Bring to a boil, then reduce the heat to a low simmer. Add the Parmesan rind (if using), bay leaves, and thyme bundle, cover, and cook, stirring occasionally, until the flavors have melded and the meat is extremely tender and flavorful, at least 4 hours (but I like to cook mine all day!).

ABOUT 30 minutes before serving, stir in the milk and continue to cook, uncovered and lightly simmering, until ready to serve. Taste and add more salt and pepper, if desired. Discard the cheese rind, bay leaves, and thyme bundle.

SERVE the sauce tossed with the pasta. If needed, add a splash of the pasta water to bring it all together and toss until glossy. Garnish with freshly grated Parmesan (if using) and fresh thyme leaves.

Chicken Dan Dan–Inspired Noodles

GLUTEN-FREE
(IF MODIFIED; SEE NOTE)
DAIRY-FREE

MAKES 4 SERVINGS • TOTAL TIME: 30 MINUTES

Anytime we dined out and dan dan noodles were on the menu, my mom ordered them so I grew to love the intensely flavorful, umami-filled noodle dish myself. While my recipe is very far from authentic, its flavors remind me of dining out with my mom, slurping up the saucy, meaty, stomach-warming noodles!

4 tablespoons avocado oil

¾ cup halved and thinly sliced shallots (about 2 shallots)

4 garlic cloves, thinly sliced

1 teaspoon crushed red pepper flakes, plus more for serving

1 pound ground chicken thigh

Kosher salt

½ teaspoon ground white pepper

½ teaspoon Chinese five-spice powder

1 teaspoon Sichuan peppercorns, crushed (I place them in a bag and crush them using the back of a spoon)

¼ cup plus 2 tablespoons coconut aminos

1 tablespoon rice vinegar

1 tablespoon freshly squeezed lime juice (about ½ lime)

1 teaspoon fish sauce

3 heads baby bok choy, leafy greens only, roughly chopped

8 ounces gluten-free linguine (I like Jovial brand brown rice pasta)

1 tablespoon gochujang (I like Mother In Law's Fermented Chile Paste Concentrate, see note)

2 tablespoons tahini

¼ cup diagonally sliced green onion, for serving

¼ cup roughly chopped roasted peanuts, for serving

1 lime, cut into wedges, for serving

PAIRING SUGGESTION: **Sesame Asparagus Sauté (page 196)**

BRING a large pot of water to a boil.

MEANWHILE, in a large deep skillet, heat 2 tablespoons of the avocado oil over medium heat. Add the shallots, garlic, and pepper flakes and cook, stirring often, until the shallots are just tender, 3 to 4 minutes. Add the chicken, 1 teaspoon salt, the white pepper, and five-spice powder and cook, breaking up the meat finely with a wooden spoon, until the chicken is cooked through, 6 to 8 minutes. Reduce the heat to medium-low.

ADD the peppercorns to the chicken mixture along with ¼ cup of the coconut aminos, the rice vinegar, lime juice, fish sauce, remaining 2 tablespoons avocado oil, and bok choy greens. Stir until well combined. Let simmer over low heat while you prepare the pasta.

MEANWHILE, add plenty of salt (about 1 tablespoon) and the pasta to the boiling water and cook until al dente, about 8 minutes (or according to the package directions). Reserve ¾ cup of the pasta water and drain the pasta.

IN a small bowl, combine the remaining 2 tablespoons coconut aminos, the gochujang, tahini, and reserved pasta water. Whisk until smooth.

TRANSFER the cooked noodles to the skillet with the chicken. Pour the tahini/gochujang mixture into the skillet and toss until the noodles are very well coated and glossy.

SERVE topped with green onions and roasted peanuts, with lime wedges on the side. Add additional pepper flakes if you like it extra spicy like me!

FROM MY KITCHEN TO YOURS

Often, gochujang is made with a small bit of wheat to help the sauce/paste firm up, making it a little difficult to find a gluten-free option. However, you can find gluten-free alternatives online and at Whole Foods. I like the Coconut Secret brand, which is coconut aminos based.

One-Pot Cacio e Pepe Israeli Couscous

MAKES 2 SERVINGS • TOTAL TIME: 25 MINUTES

Cacio e pepe is one of the simple pleasures in life, and just happens to be one of my favorite foods on planet Earth. Translating literally as "cheese and pepper" and traditionally served with spaghetti, the dish tastes like it's loaded with butter and cream—but it's not; it's all about the technique. The ingredient list is deceptively short, but it takes pan-sauce-making precision to get it just right. I really love Israeli couscous for its soft, slightly chewy texture and the starch it creates when cooked down in water, so I experimented and created this one-pot Israeli couscous version! The couscous adds a nice, creamy texture, making it the perfect candidate for a faux cacio e pepe that is foolproof in the kitchen.

1½ cups Israeli or pearl couscous

1 teaspoon kosher salt

2 teaspoons freshly ground black pepper

⅓ cup freshly grated pecorino cheese or Parmigiano-Reggiano, plus more for serving

1½ cups roughly chopped baby arugula, optional

1 teaspoon finely chopped fresh parsley

IN a medium pot, combine the Israeli couscous and 3 cups water. Bring to a boil over high heat. Reduce the heat to a light simmer and cook uncovered, stirring occasionally, until the liquid has been absorbed and the couscous is tender, about 10 minutes.

REMOVE the pot from the heat. Season the couscous with the salt and 1 teaspoon of the pepper. Stir in the pecorino. Add the arugula, if using, and toss until the arugula is slightly wilted and just combined.

DIVIDE the couscous between two bowls and top each bowl with ½ teaspoon pepper and a sprinkle of freshly grated pecorino cheese and the parsley. Serve immediately.

Herby Green Olive Pasta with Feta

|| GLUTEN-FREE (IF MODIFIED)

MAKES 4 SERVINGS • TOTAL TIME: 25 MINUTES

I am an olive lover through and through, but none are as delicious as Castelvetrano olives, in my opinion one of the best gifts that God gave to this earth. While other olives can have a mushy texture and can be overly salty, Castelvetrano olives have a lovely firm texture and mild flavor. While they are firm in texture, when you take a bite of them, they taste creamy and buttery. Ah, perfection.

I always keep these beautiful bright-green olives in my pantry to throw on charcuterie boards or in dishes for an extra bite of flavor. When sautéed with pancetta, garlic, and red pepper flakes, they become even more magical. Toss that mixture into pasta with some bright lemon, feta cheese, and fresh dill and you have a restaurant-worthy pasta dish. Yum!

8 ounces linguine (sub brown rice pasta for gluten-free)

Kosher salt

4 ounces diced pancetta

4 garlic cloves, minced

½ teaspoon crushed red pepper flakes

Grated zest of ½ lemon

1 cup halved pitted Castelvetrano olives

2 tablespoons chopped fresh parsley leaves, plus more for serving

2 tablespoons chopped fresh basil leaves, plus more for serving

2 tablespoons chopped fresh dill fronds, plus more for serving

6 ounces feta cheese, cut into medium dice

2 tablespoons freshly squeezed lemon juice (about 1 lemon)

¼ cup panko bread crumbs (I use Aleia's gluten-free panko bread crumbs)

1 lemon, cut into wedges, for serving

BRING a large pot of water to a boil. Add the pasta with plenty of salt (about 1 tablespoon) and stir. Cook according to the package directions.

WHEN the pasta has about 8 minutes left to cook, in a large deep skillet, cook the pancetta over medium heat until crisp, about 5 minutes. Transfer the browned pancetta to a plate lined with paper towels. Drain the excess fat from the pan, reserving 2 tablespoons in the pan.

ADD the garlic, pepper flakes, and lemon zest to the pan and cook, stirring often, until the garlic is fragrant and lightly browned, about 2 minutes. Add the olives, parsley, basil, and dill and cook, stirring often, until the olives have softened and the pasta is ready.

RESERVE ½ cup of the pasta water and set aside. Drain the pasta and add it to the skillet along with the pancetta and toss to coat. Increase the heat to medium-high. Add about two-thirds of the diced feta (reserving the remaining for serving), the lemon juice, and ¼ cup of the reserved pasta water. Cook, tossing the pasta, until the feta has just melted. If the pasta looks dry, add the remaining ¼ cup pasta water and toss until well coated and glossy. Add ½ teaspoon salt and the panko and toss once more to combine. Taste and add more salt, if desired.

SERVE in bowls and garnish with the remaining diced feta, more chopped herbs, and a wedge of lemon.

One-Pot Cajun Chicken Pasta

MAKES 4 SERVINGS • TOTAL TIME: 25 MINUTES

1 teaspoon paprika

½ teaspoon cayenne pepper (see note)

½ teaspoon dried thyme

½ teaspoon dried rosemary

½ teaspoon dried oregano

1 teaspoon kosher salt, plus more to taste

½ teaspoon freshly ground black pepper, plus more to taste

1 pound boneless, skinless chicken breasts

2 tablespoons extra-virgin olive oil, plus more as needed

½ cup small-diced white onion (about ½ small onion)

2 garlic cloves, minced

12 ounces brown rice penne pasta (I like Jovial brand)

2 cups (16 ounces) low-sodium chicken broth

2 cups whole milk (sub almond milk for dairy-free)

2 tablespoons freshly squeezed lemon juice (about 1 lemon)

1 Roma (plum) tomato, seeded and minced

4 thinly sliced green onions, green parts only

¼ cup freshly shredded Parmesan cheese, optional (omit for dairy-free)

FROM MY KITCHEN TO YOURS

Just ½ teaspoon of cayenne is spicy! For a milder flavor, go for ¼ teaspoon. If you're serving kids, omit it altogether.

Okay, who grew up eating at Chili's Grill & Bar? Well, let's just say I grew up eating there a little too often. I think I tried just about everything on the menu during my teen years and absolutely loved it all. One of my favorite orders was Chili's Cajun Chicken Pasta. It was the creamiest, cheesiest pasta dish topped with Cajun-crusted chicken and a giant slice of Texas-style garlic toast. Whoa—so dang good. Here, I've lightened up that recipe in an easy, one-pot pasta dish. You won't believe how delicious this pasta is with minimal effort. It's got big, bold Cajun spices and a lovely, creamy sauce.

IN a small bowl, combine the paprika, cayenne, thyme, rosemary, oregano, salt, and pepper. Stir until well combined and set aside.

PLACE the chicken breasts on a cutting board and cover with parchment or plastic wrap. Using a meat mallet or the bottom of a heavy skillet, pound the chicken to a uniform ¼-inch thickness. Pat the chicken dry with a paper towel.

SEASON the chicken on both sides with 2 teaspoons of the prepared spice blend.

IN a large deep skillet, heat the oil over medium-high heat. When hot, add the chicken and sear until golden brown on both sides and cooked through, 3 to 4 minutes per side. Transfer the cooked chicken to a cutting board and let it rest while you make the pasta.

REDUCE the heat under the pan to medium. Add the onion and garlic and sauté, scraping up any browned bits and stirring until tender, about 3 minutes.

ADD the pasta, chicken broth, milk, and the remaining spice blend. Bring to a gentle simmer (you don't want it to boil) and cook, stirring often, until the pasta is al dente and the liquid is absorbed and creamy, 12 to 15 minutes.

MEANWHILE, slice the chicken into ½-inch strips against the grain.

ADD the lemon juice to the pasta, taste, and add salt and pepper to taste, as desired. Serve in bowls and top with the sliced chicken, tomato, green onion, and Parmesan (if using).

vegetarian dinners

Eggplant Lasagna

MAKES 8 SERVINGS • TOTAL TIME: 1 HOUR 10 MINUTES

2 large (8-inch-long) eggplants or 3 medium eggplants (see note)

2 tablespoons extra-virgin olive oil

1½ teaspoons kosher salt

15 ounces whole-milk ricotta cheese

2 large eggs, whisked

1 cup freshly shredded Parmesan cheese

1 cup freshly shredded mozzarella cheese

½ cup finely chopped fresh parsley, plus more, optional for garnish

2 tablespoons fresh thyme leaves

1 teaspoon grated lemon zest

½ teaspoon freshly ground black pepper

½ teaspoon crushed red pepper flakes

One 24-ounce jar arrabbiata sauce (I like Rao's brand; see note)

FROM MY KITCHEN TO YOURS

EGGPLANT SIZE: Eggplants vary in size! If you find only medium eggplants (under 8 inches), you'll definitely need three or you won't have enough for a top layer.

SPICE LEVEL: Don't want it spicy? Use a classic jarred marinara instead of arrabbiata sauce. While I prefer it with the arrabbiata sauce, my kiddos prefer it with marinara. A lot of times I make it with marinara, then just cover my serving with red pepper flakes for a spicy kick!

As far as meatless meals go, I'll admit it's hard to beat this vegetarian lasagna. Eggplant makes the perfect veggie substitute for noodles in this flavorful, delicious, and easy lasagna recipe that will have everyone at the table talking! I made this for a group of Clayton's friends once just to see what they'd think, and they all couldn't believe it was made with eggplant. They proceeded to devour the entire dish!

PREHEAT the oven to 400°F. Line two sheet pans with parchment paper.

CUT off and discard the ends of the eggplant. Slice the eggplant lengthwise into ¼-inch-thick "lasagna noodles." It is easiest to do this by first cutting the eggplant in half lengthwise, then, working with one half at a time, place the eggplant cut side down on a cutting board, and use a sharp knife, with steady strokes, to slice the eggplant lengthwise into long, thin slices.

PLACE the sliced eggplant in a single layer on the prepared sheet pans. Brush the eggplant slices on both sides with the olive oil and sprinkle with 1 teaspoon salt. Transfer to the oven and roast until golden and lightly crisp on the edges, 15 to 17 minutes.

MEANWHILE, in a large bowl, combine the ricotta, eggs, Parmesan, ¼ cup of the mozzarella, the parsley, 1 tablespoon of the thyme, the lemon zest, black pepper, pepper flakes, and remaining ½ teaspoon salt. Stir until well combined and set aside.

SPREAD ¾ cup of the arrabbiata sauce in an even layer in a 2½-quart oval baking dish or 9 × 13-inch baking dish. Place a single layer of the roasted eggplant over the sauce. Spread half of the ricotta mixture on top, followed by ¾ cup of the arrabbiata sauce.

REPEAT the layers with a single layer of roasted eggplant, the remaining ricotta mixture, and ¾ cup of the arrabbiata sauce.

FOR the last layer, top with the remaining eggplant slices and the remaining arrabbiata sauce and sprinkle with the remaining ¾ cup mozzarella.

BAKE, uncovered, until the cheese is bubbling and lightly browned, 20 to 23 minutes. Set aside to cool for 10 minutes, then slice and serve. Garnish with parsley if desired.

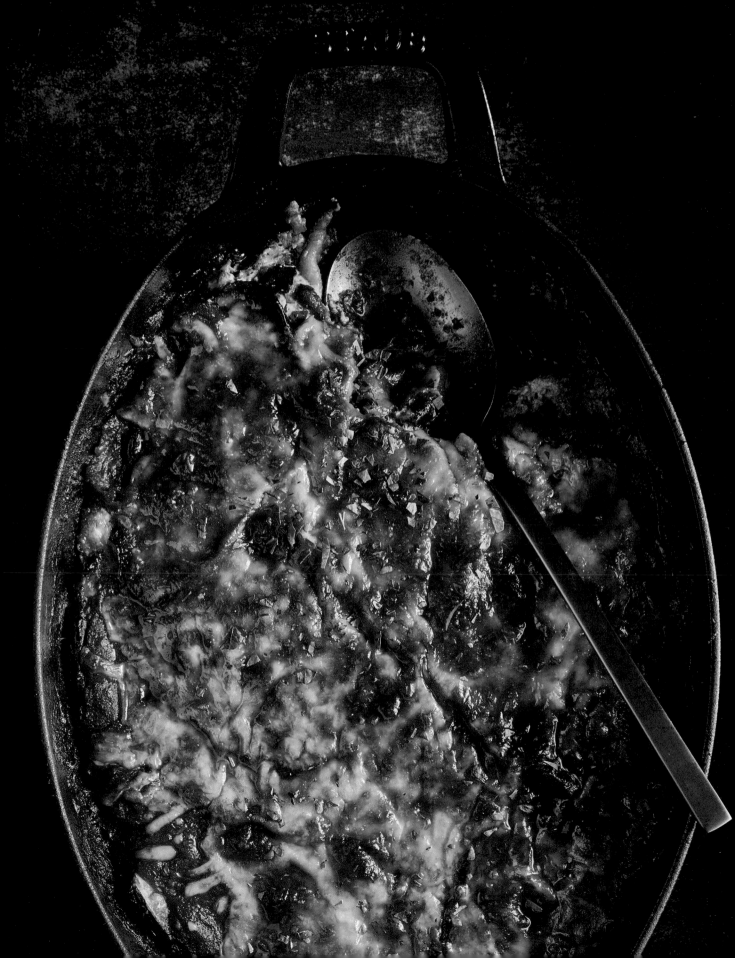

Fried Avocado Tacos with Spicy Crema

MAKES 4 SERVINGS • TOTAL TIME: 25 MINUTES

FOR THE SPICY CREMA

2 tablespoons Homemade Mayo (page 251)

2 tablespoons sriracha hot sauce

1 tablespoon freshly squeezed lime juice (about ½ lime)

1 garlic clove, minced

1 teaspoon honey

Pinch of kosher salt

Pinch of freshly ground black pepper

FOR THE SLAW

One 7.5-ounce bag coleslaw mix

½ teaspoon toasted sesame oil

1 tablespoon avocado oil

1 tablespoon rice vinegar

¼ teaspoon kosher salt

¼ teaspoon freshly ground black pepper

FOR THE FRIED AVOCADO

1 large egg, whisked

½ cup gluten-free panko bread crumbs

2 tablespoons white sesame seeds

1 tablespoon black sesame seeds

1 teaspoon kosher salt, plus more for finishing

½ teaspoon freshly ground black pepper

¼ teaspoon cayenne pepper, optional

¼ cup avocado oil, plus more as needed for frying

2 large ripe but still firm avocados, cut into ½-inch-thick wedges

When I lived in Austin, Texas, I used to love going to Mighty Cone—a food truck known for its delicious fried avocado tacos. They are crispy on the outside, creamy on the inside, and just irresistible. I've done my own little at-home rendition of their avocado tacos, and it's a recipe I know you're all going to eat up! I love the toasted sesame and panko crunch combined with the simple slaw and sriracha aioli—YUM!

MAKE THE SPICY CREMA: In a small bowl, combine the spicy crema ingredients and stir until well combined. Set aside.

MAKE THE SLAW: In a large bowl, combine all the slaw ingredients and toss until well combined. Set aside.

MAKE THE FRIED AVOCADO: Place the egg in a shallow bowl. In a separate shallow bowl, combine the panko, white and black sesame seeds, salt, pepper, and cayenne (if using). Stir to combine.

IN a large nonstick skillet, heat the avocado oil over medium heat.

MEANWHILE, dip each of the avocado wedges in the egg wash, then gently roll in the panko mixture until evenly coated, making sure to coat all sides.

GENTLY place the avocado slices in the hot oil. Cook until golden brown on both sides, about 2 minutes per side, including the back of the wedge. You may need to work in batches to avoid crowding the pan. If needed, clean out the pan between batches and add a bit more oil. Transfer the cooked avocado wedges to a plate lined with paper towels.

TO SERVE: One at a time, place the tortillas in a dry (no oil) stainless steel skillet over medium heat and cook for about 30 seconds on each side. You can also do away with the skillet and char the tortillas directly over a gas flame for a few seconds using tongs.

TO build each taco, place the slaw in a warm tortilla, then add 2 or 3 fried avocado wedges, a drizzle of the spicy crema, a few pickled onions (if using), cilantro, serrano (if using), and a squeeze of lime.

FOR SERVING

8 grain-free tortillas (I use Siete brand)

Quick-Pickled Red Onions (page 248), optional

¼ cup chopped fresh cilantro

½ serrano pepper, very thinly sliced, optional

1 lime, cut into wedges

FROM MY KITCHEN TO YOURS

The best way to slice an avocado is to cut it in half, remove the pit, peel, and slice.

Harissa- and Farro-Stuffed Acorn Squash

MAKES 4 SERVINGS • TOTAL TIME: 40 MINUTES

Roasted acorn squash is the perfect edible bowl to fill with whatever you can dream up. What's not to love about this versatile and flavorful veggie? In this recipe, I've used one of my favorite pantry staples, harissa, a Tunisian hot chile pepper paste, to add heat and extra flavor to this nourishing vegetarian dinner. I love the firm, plump, and characteristically chewy farro alone, but in this dish, its nutty flavor stands up perfectly to the sweetness of the dried cranberries and earthy acorn squash, making this dish a home run!

FOR THE ACORN SQUASH

2 medium acorn squash

2 tablespoons extra-virgin olive oil

½ teaspoon kosher salt

FOR THE FILLING

2 tablespoons extra-virgin olive oil

¼ cup minced yellow onion (about ¼ small onion)

2 garlic cloves, minced

1 cup farro

Grated zest of ½ lemon

½ teaspoon ground coriander

½ teaspoon ground cumin

1 teaspoon kosher salt

2 teaspoons mild harissa

2 cups (16 ounces) low-sodium vegetable broth

⅓ cup dried cranberries

⅓ cup roasted pumpkin seeds

¼ cup roughly chopped fresh mint leaves

¼ cup roughly chopped fresh cilantro leaves

2 tablespoons freshly squeezed lemon juice (about 1 lemon)

3 cups baby arugula

PREHEAT the oven to 375°F. Line a large sheet pan with parchment paper.

BAKE THE ACORN SQUASH: Trim the ends of the squash, halve them crosswise, and scoop out the seeds. Place the squash cut side up on the baking sheet and brush the flesh with the olive oil to evenly coat. Sprinkle with the salt. Bake until the flesh of the squash is fork-tender, 30 to 35 minutes.

MEANWHILE, MAKE THE FILLING: In a large sauté pan, heat the oil over medium heat. Add the onion and garlic and cook, stirring often, until softened, about 4 minutes. Add the farro, lemon zest, coriander, cumin, and salt and cook until the farro is lightly toasted, about 3 minutes. Stir in the harissa and vegetable broth and bring to a boil. Reduce the heat to a simmer and cook uncovered, stirring often, until the farro is tender but not mushy, about 20 minutes. Stir in the dried cranberries, pumpkin seeds, mint, cilantro, and lemon juice until well combined.

WHEN the squash is ready to be stuffed, toss the baby arugula with the farro mixture until just combined and slightly wilted. Immediately stuff the farro mixture into the cavity of each squash half and serve.

Mongolian Mushrooms

MAKES 4 SERVINGS • TOTAL TIME: 15 MINUTES

4 large portobello mushrooms

2 tablespoons plus ¼ cup avocado oil

2 teaspoons tapioca flour

6 green onions, cut into 2-inch lengths

2 teaspoons toasted sesame oil

½ cup coconut aminos

2 teaspoons fish sauce (optional; non-vegetarian)

2 teaspoons rice vinegar

½ teaspoon crushed red pepper flakes

½ teaspoon ground ginger

½ teaspoon ground white pepper

2 tablespoons toasted sesame seeds

¼ cup low-sodium vegetable broth or water

Kosher salt, to taste

Prepared cauliflower rice or steamed rice, optional for serving

Here is a fun veggie take inspired by the oh-so-popular dish Mongolian beef. I love how hearty the mushrooms are in this dish, and how they absorb all the delicious flavors in the sauce. It also comes together in just 15 minutes, making it one of my absolute favorite Meatless Monday meals! Since mushrooms absorb a lot of liquid, make sure you serve the dish immediately after it's finished to keep their texture.

CLEAN the mushrooms well and pat dry. Remove the stems and discard. Cut the mushroom caps into ½-inch-thick slices. Cut the longer pieces in half crosswise so that each piece is about 2 inches long.

PLACE the sliced mushrooms in a large bowl with 2 tablespoons of the avocado oil and toss to coat evenly. Add the tapioca flour and toss to coat again.

IN a large nonstick skillet, heat the remaining ¼ cup avocado oil over medium-high heat. Working in two batches, place the mushrooms in a single layer and cook until golden brown, about 2 minutes per side. Transfer the cooked mushrooms to a plate and repeat.

RETURN the cooked mushrooms to the skillet and add the green onions, sesame oil, coconut aminos, fish sauce (if using), rice vinegar, pepper flakes, ginger, white pepper, sesame seeds, and broth. Cook, stirring often, until the sauce has thickened and the green onions are just tender, 2 to 3 minutes. Taste and add salt, if needed.

IF desired, serve with prepared rice.

Red Lentil Chili

MAKES 4 SERVINGS • TOTAL TIME: 45 MINUTES

GLUTEN-FREE (IF MODIFIED)
DAIRY-FREE (IF MODIFIED)
VEGETARIAN

Have you ever found yourself at home, hungry, and with zero motivation (or time) to go to the grocery store? Yeah, happens all the time. This is when I love making magic with what I have in my pantry. As a born-and-raised Texan, a beefy, hearty chili has always been one of my favorite comfort foods. Here, I swap the meat out for lentils, and it is delicious.

2 tablespoons avocado oil

2 cups minced yellow onion (about 1 large onion)

1 cup minced seeded poblano pepper (about 1 large poblano)

4 garlic cloves, minced

2 cups red lentils

2 tablespoons chili powder

2 teaspoons smoked paprika

1 teaspoon ground cumin

½ teaspoon cayenne pepper, optional

2 teaspoons kosher salt

1 teaspoon freshly ground black pepper

3 tablespoons tomato paste

2 cups (16 ounces) light beer (I recommend Modelo; sub gluten-free beer for gluten-free)

4 cups (32 ounces) low-sodium vegetable broth

1 bay leaf

One 14.5-ounce can diced fire-roasted tomatoes

OPTIONAL GARNISHES

¼ cup plain Greek yogurt or sour cream (omit for dairy-free)

¼ cup crumbled corn chips

¼ cup shredded Mexican cheese blend (omit for dairy-free)

2 tablespoons chopped fresh cilantro

1 lime, cut into wedges

1 jalapeño, thinly sliced

IN a large pot or Dutch oven, heat the oil over medium heat. Add the onion, poblano, and garlic and cook, stirring often, until the veggies are just tender, 5 to 7 minutes.

ADD the lentils, chili powder, smoked paprika, cumin, cayenne, salt, and black pepper and cook, stirring often until the spices are fragrant and lightly toasted, about 2 minutes.

ADD the tomato paste and 1 cup of the beer and continue to cook, stirring, until the tomato paste is incorporated and the beer evaporates, about 2 minutes. Add the remaining 1 cup beer, the vegetable broth, bay leaf, and diced tomatoes and stir to combine. Bring to a boil and reduce the heat to a simmer. Cover the pot and cook until the lentils are tender, about 15 minutes.

UNCOVER and simmer, stirring often, to let the liquid reduce a bit more, about 5 minutes. Discard the bay leaf.

DIVIDE the chili among four bowls. Serve as is or with desired garnishes.

Roasted Veggie Enchiladas Verdes

MAKES 4 SERVINGS • TOTAL TIME: 1 HOUR

FOR THE VEGGIES

4 cups small cauliflower florets (about 1 small head)

2 cups medium-diced zucchini (about 1 large zucchini)

1 cup medium-diced seeded poblano pepper (about 1 poblano)

2 tablespoons avocado oil

1 teaspoon kosher salt

¼ teaspoon freshly ground black pepper

FOR THE GREEN ENCHILADA SAUCE

1 tablespoon avocado oil

1 cup medium-diced white onion (about ½ large onion)

¼ cup medium-diced seeded jalapeño (about 1 large jalapeño)

3 garlic cloves, peeled

1 teaspoon ground cumin

1 teaspoon onion powder

1 teaspoon garlic powder

Four 4-ounce cans mild diced green chiles

1 tablespoon apple cider vinegar

½ cup low-sodium vegetable broth

1 teaspoon kosher salt

FOR THE ENCHILADAS

One 15-ounce can black beans, drained and rinsed

1½ cups freshly shredded Monterey Jack cheese

8 grain-free tortillas (I use Siete brand)

Roughly chopped fresh cilantro leaves, optional for serving

Flaky salt, optional for serving

This recipe speaks for itself. Filled with beautiful roasted veggies and black beans, then smothered in an easy green enchilada sauce, these are the ultimate veggie enchiladas.

PREHEAT the oven to 375°F. Line a large sheet pan with parchment paper.

ROAST THE VEGETABLES: Place the cauliflower florets, zucchini, and poblano pepper on the lined sheet pan. Drizzle with the avocado oil, season with the salt and pepper, and toss until well combined. Spread the vegetables into an even layer and bake until the cauliflower is golden brown and tender, 18 to 20 minutes.

MEANWHILE, MAKE THE GREEN ENCHILADA SAUCE: In a medium saucepan, heat the avocado oil over medium heat. Add the onion, jalapeño, garlic, cumin, onion powder, and garlic powder and cook, stirring often, until the onion and jalapeño are tender and the spices are fragrant, 5 to 7 minutes.

TRANSFER the sautéed onion/jalapeño mixture to a food processor or blender with the diced green chiles, vinegar, vegetable broth, and salt. Blend until smooth and set aside.

FOR THE ENCHILADAS: When the vegetables are done roasting, pour the black beans and ½ cup of the green enchilada sauce over the roasted veggies on the pan. Gently toss until well combined. Add 1 cup of the Monterey Jack and toss the filling until well combined.

TO assemble, spread 1 cup of the green enchilada sauce in a 9 × 13-inch baking dish to evenly coat the bottom.

ONE at a time, place the tortillas in a dry (no oil) stainless steel skillet over medium heat and warm for about 30 seconds on each side to make them more pliable. You can also do away with the skillet and char the tortillas directly over a gas flame for a few seconds using tongs. Fill each warmed tortilla with about ⅓ cup of the filling, gently roll it up, and place it seam side down in the baking dish.

POUR the remaining sauce over the enchiladas. Sprinkle any leftover filling down the center of the enchiladas. Top with the remaining ½ cup Monterey Jack.

COVER with foil and bake for 15 minutes. Remove the foil and bake until the cheese is golden brown, 8 to 10 minutes.

GARNISH with cilantro and flaky salt, if desired.

Honey-Sesame Sheet Pan Cauliflower

MAKES 2 SERVINGS • TOTAL TIME: 30 MINUTES

1 large head cauliflower, cut into bite-size florets (about 6 cups)

¼ cup avocado oil

1 teaspoon kosher salt

1 teaspoon white sesame seeds, plus more for garnish

1 teaspoon toasted sesame oil

¼ cup coconut aminos

1 teaspoon fish sauce (optional; non-vegetarian)

1 teaspoon rice vinegar

¼ cup honey

¼ cup low-sodium vegetable broth

2 garlic cloves, minced

1-inch piece fresh ginger, peeled and grated

1 teaspoon arrowroot flour

¼ cup seeded and roughly chopped Fresno chiles (about 2 small chiles)

Steamed rice, optional for serving

2 tablespoons finely chopped fresh cilantro or Thai basil, for serving

In this meatless meal, cauliflower gets promoted from a side dish to the main dish! I love how easy and flavorful this sheet pan cauliflower "stir-fry" is. It's sweet, savory, and a little spicy from the Fresno chile. Served over a bowl of steamed rice, this is a veggie dish that any hungry foodie can get behind!

PREHEAT the oven to 450°F. Line a sheet pan with parchment paper.

SPREAD the cauliflower on the lined pan. Drizzle with the avocado oil and sprinkle with the salt. Toss until the cauliflower is well coated in the oil. Spread into an even layer and roast for 10 minutes.

MEANWHILE, heat a small saucepan over medium heat. Add the sesame seeds and cook, stirring often, until the seeds are fragrant and lightly toasted, 1 to 2 minutes. Add the sesame oil, coconut aminos, fish sauce (if using), rice vinegar, honey, vegetable broth, garlic, and ginger and stir to combine.

IN a small bowl, make a slurry by combining the arrowroot flour and 1 tablespoon water. Whisk until well combined. While stirring the sauce, slowly add the slurry to the saucepan and cook, stirring often, until the sauce thickens, about 5 minutes. Remove from the heat and set aside.

ADD the Fresno chiles to the sheet pan with the roasted cauliflower and toss. Roast until the chiles are softened and the cauliflower is golden brown, 6 to 10 minutes.

POUR the sauce over the cauliflower mixture and gently toss until the cauliflower is well coated. Spread into an even layer and roast for 2 to 3 minutes to allow the sauce to caramelize over the cauliflower.

SERVE over rice (if using) and garnish with sesame seeds and cilantro or Thai basil. Serve immediately!

Spaghetti Squash Singapore Noodles

MAKES 4 SERVINGS • TOTAL TIME: 50 MINUTES

Have you ever had Singapore noodles? It's a fantastic curried rice noodle dish that typically contains shrimp, pork, and vegetables. I love ordering it when I see it on a menu! Inspired by the dish, I subbed spaghetti squash for the rice noodles, and I knew it was a winner when my husband and his coworkers devoured the entire platter. This is definitely one of my favorite ways to sneak veggies in on any day of the week! For a fast weeknight dish, make the spaghetti squash ahead of time and the whole recipe will come together in less than 20 minutes.

FOR THE SPAGHETTI SQUASH

1 medium spaghetti squash (2 to 3 pounds)

2 tablespoons avocado oil

½ teaspoon kosher salt

FOR THE VEGETABLES

2 tablespoons avocado oil

2 large eggs, whisked

1 teaspoon toasted sesame oil

3 garlic cloves, thinly sliced

3 dried Thai red chiles, stemmed and halved lengthwise, or ¼ teaspoon cayenne pepper or more to taste

1 cup matchstick carrots

½ cup halved and thinly sliced red onion

2 cups thinly sliced napa cabbage

1 teaspoon kosher salt, plus more to taste

½ teaspoon freshly ground black pepper

4 green onions, sliced on the diagonal into 2-inch lengths, plus more for garnish

4 teaspoons curry powder

¼ cup coconut aminos

2 teaspoons fish sauce (optional; non-vegetarian)

1 tablespoon rice vinegar

1 lime, cut into wedges, for serving

PREHEAT the oven to 400°F. Line a sheet pan with parchment paper.

MAKE THE SPAGHETTI SQUASH: Trim the ends of the spaghetti squash and halve it crosswise. Using a sharp spoon or ice cream scoop, scoop out the seeds and stringy bits from the center of each cavity and discard. Brush the inside of the halves all over with the avocado oil and sprinkle with the salt. Place the squash cut side down on the lined sheet pan and roast until fork-tender, 35 to 40 minutes. Set aside until cool enough to handle.

USING a fork, gently scrape out the strands so that they resemble spaghetti and set aside.

MAKE THE VEGETABLES: In a skillet, heat 1 tablespoon of the avocado oil over medium heat. Pour the eggs into the skillet, swirl them around to coat the bottom of the pan and let them set like an omelet, without stirring, about 2 minutes. Fold the eggs over themselves and, using a spatula, dice them up. Transfer the omelet pieces to a plate and set aside.

IN the same skillet, increase the heat to medium-high and add the remaining tablespoon of avocado oil, the sesame oil, garlic, red chiles, carrots, red onion, napa cabbage, salt, and pepper. Cook, stirring often, until the veggies are slightly tender, about 3 minutes.

ADD the spaghetti squash, green onions, curry powder, coconut aminos, fish sauce (if using), and rice vinegar and cook, tossing until the spaghetti squash is well coated in the sauce, 2 to 3 minutes. Add the diced egg and toss to combine.

TASTE and add more salt if desired. Serve with lime wedges and garnish with green onions.

beef, pork, and lamb

Steak au Poivre

MAKE 2 SERVINGS • TOTAL TIME: 40 MINUTES

Pan-seared filet mignon with a crunchy peppercorn crust and rich Cognac sauce is a classic French dish. I've given it a little twist using ingredients that I always have on hand in my kitchen and subbed in sherry vinegar instead of cognac to keep the dish paleo compatible. Whether you're making this dish for a special weekend treat or for an at-home Valentine's Day, it's sure to make your date night feel special.

FOR THE STEAKS

2 teaspoons black peppercorns

2 filet mignon steaks (6 to 8 ounces each)

1½ teaspoons kosher salt, plus more to taste

1 tablespoon avocado oil

FOR THE AU POIVRE SAUCE

1 tablespoon ghee or unsalted butter (sub vegan butter for dairy-free)

¼ cup finely minced shallot (about 1 large shallot)

2 garlic cloves, minced

1 teaspoon Dijon mustard

1 tablespoon sherry vinegar

¼ cup low-sodium beef broth

½ cup unsweetened full-fat coconut milk

1 teaspoon finely chopped fresh thyme leaves, plus more for garnish

PAIRING SUGGESTIONS: Apple Cider Vinegar and Dijon Roasted Root Vegetables (page 207), Zesty Potato Wedges (page 210), Little Gem Salad with Lemon Dressing (page 204)

MAKE THE STEAKS: Place the peppercorns in a small zip-top plastic bag and place on a cutting board. Using a meat mallet or the bottom of a heavy skillet, coarsely crush the peppercorns.

PAT the steaks very dry with a paper towel. Season them on all sides with the salt and 1 teaspoon of the crushed peppercorns, reserving the rest for the sauce. Press the seasoning into the steaks, massaging it into the surface. Set aside and let the steaks rest at room temperature for 15 minutes.

MEANWHILE, in a large skillet (preferably cast iron), heat the avocado oil over medium-high heat until the oil just begins to shimmer but not smoke. Carefully transfer the steaks to the skillet and sear undisturbed until a deep-brown crust forms on each side, about 4 minutes per side for medium-rare or 5 to 6 minutes per side for well-done. Transfer the steaks to a cutting board to rest while you make the sauce.

MAKE THE AU POIVRE SAUCE: Remove the skillet from the heat and let it cool a bit, about 2 minutes. If there are any burned bits in the skillet, wipe it clean with a paper towel. Return the skillet to medium heat. Add the ghee, let it melt, then add the shallot and garlic. Cook, stirring often, until the shallot is tender and the garlic is fragrant, 1 to 2 minutes. Stir in the mustard, sherry vinegar, and broth until well combined and bring to a rapid simmer. Using the side of a spoon, scrape up any browned bits. Stir in the coconut milk, thyme, and reserved crushed peppercorns and simmer, stirring often, until the sauce has thickened, about 4 minutes. Taste the sauce and add a pinch of salt, if desired.

PLATE the steaks and spoon the sauce over the top. Garnish with fresh thyme. Serve immediately.

Cumin Beef Stir-Fry

MAKE 4 SERVINGS • TOTAL TIME: 45 MINUTES

If you've gone your entire life without trying Sichuan peppercorns, let's put an end to that with this dish. This fragrant beef stir-fry is inspired by one of my favorite Sichuan-style restaurants, Mala Sichuan Bistro, located in Houston, Texas—it's a must-go any time I pass through. A dish we always order is their Cumin Lamb, a stir-fry filled with chiles, onions, and, of course, the lovely tingle from Sichuan peppercorns. It's a dish that will blow your mind and make your taste buds jump for joy!

FOR THE STEAK

1½ pounds flank steak

1 teaspoon avocado oil

1 tablespoon coconut aminos

1 teaspoon kosher salt

½ teaspoon freshly ground black pepper

2 teaspoons tapioca flour

FOR THE STIR-FRY

2 tablespoons avocado oil, plus more as needed

1 teaspoon toasted sesame oil

½ cup halved and thinly sliced white onion (about ½ medium onion)

½ teaspoon crushed red pepper flakes

1½ teaspoons freshly ground Sichuan peppercorns (see note)

1½ teaspoons ground cumin

6 garlic cloves, thinly sliced

¼ cup coconut aminos

2 teaspoons fish sauce

1 tablespoon rice vinegar

4 green onions, green parts only, cut into 2-inch lengths

Prepared cauliflower rice or steamed rice, optional for serving

PAIRING SUGGESTION: Sesame Asparagus Sauté (page 196)

PREPARE THE STEAK: Place the steak on a cutting board. Using a meat mallet or the bottom of a heavy skillet, pound the steak to an even ¼-inch thickness. Cutting against the grain, slice the steak into ¼-inch-wide strips that are about 3 inches long. Place the sliced steak in a large bowl and add the avocado oil, coconut aminos, salt, pepper, and tapioca flour. Toss until well combined. Set aside to marinate at room temperature for 15 to 20 minutes.

MAKE THE STIR-FRY: Heat a large wok or skillet over medium-high heat with the avocado oil. Working in batches to keep from crowding the skillet, sear the beef until a golden-brown crust begins to form, about 2 minutes per side. Transfer the cooked beef to a plate and continue cooking the rest of the beef. If the skillet runs dry as you're stir frying the meat, add more oil as needed.

WHEN the meat is cooked, add another teaspoon of avocado oil if the skillet is dry and the sesame oil. Add the onion, pepper flakes, ground Sichuan peppercorns, cumin, and garlic and cook until fragrant, 1 to 2 minutes, stirring often and scraping up any browned bits. Take care not to burn the garlic!

RETURN the beef and its juices to the pan and toss until well coated in the spices. Add the coconut aminos, fish sauce, rice vinegar, and half of the green onions. Stir to combine.

COOK, stirring, until the sauce has just thickened, 2 to 3 minutes. Top with the rest of the green onions and serve alone or with prepared rice.

FROM MY KITCHEN TO YOURS

I grind my Sichuan peppercorns in a spice grinder, but you can also just throw them in a zip-top bag and crush them with the bottom of a skillet.

Epic Baked Meatballs

MAKES 6 SERVINGS • TOTAL TIME: 1 HOUR 30 MINUTES (MOSTLY UNATTENDED)

This recipe has been one of the most popular posts on my blog for years, with good reason! The cashews in the meatballs give them perfect texture while the basil adds a vibrant, explosive flavor, taking these meatballs to, well, epic status. I love making this recipe for friends in need of a home-cooked meal! The cook time is long but it keeps the meatballs tender. Using a store-bought marinara, like Rao's, makes these a breeze.

1 tablespoon extra-virgin olive oil, for greasing the pan

1 cup packed fresh basil leaves, plus more for serving

3 garlic cloves, peeled

½ cup raw cashews

Grated zest of 1 lemon

2 slices no-sugar-added bacon (I like Applegate brand), minced

1 pound ground beef

1 pound ground pork

1½ teaspoons kosher salt

½ teaspoon freshly ground black pepper

½ teaspoon crushed red pepper flakes, optional

½ teaspoon dried oregano

2 tablespoons arrowroot flour

2 large eggs, whisked

One 32-ounce jar marinara sauce (I like Rao's brand)

2 tablespoons chopped fresh flat-leaf parsley, for serving

Roasted spaghetti squash or gluten-free pasta, optional for serving

PAIRING SUGGESTION: Little Gem Salad with Lemon Dressing (page 204)

PREHEAT the oven to 425°F. Use a paper towel to evenly coat the bottom of a 9 × 13-inch baking dish with the olive oil.

IN a food processor or blender, process the basil and garlic until finely chopped. Add the cashews and lemon zest and process until the cashews are finely chopped. The mixture should have a crumbly, dough-like consistency.

TRANSFER the cashew/basil mixture to a large bowl and add the bacon, beef, pork, salt, black pepper, pepper flakes, oregano, arrowroot flour, and eggs. Using clean hands, mix the meat until well combined.

USING your hands, form the meat mixture into 2-inch balls. Place the meatballs in a single layer in the prepared baking dish. There should be about 18 meatballs.

BAKE, uncovered, until the meatballs are browned, about 20 minutes.

DRAIN off any excess fat and reduce the oven temperature to 325°F. Pour the marinara evenly over the meatballs, return to the oven, and bake, uncovered, until the meatballs are tender and the sauce is very hot and bubbling, about 45 minutes.

LET cool for 5 to 10 minutes before serving. Garnish with basil and parsley. I love to serve mine over roasted spaghetti squash or gluten-free pasta!

Spiced Lamb Lettuce Cups with Tzatziki

GLUTEN-FREE
GRAIN-FREE

MAKES 4 SERVINGS • TOTAL TIME: 30 MINUTES

FOR THE TZATZIKI

6 ounces (¾ cup) plain 2% or whole-milk Greek yogurt

2 tablespoons extra-virgin olive oil

1 cup minced Persian (mini) cucumber

1 tablespoon finely chopped fresh dill

3 garlic cloves, minced

½ teaspoon distilled white vinegar

2 tablespoons freshly squeezed lemon juice (about 1 lemon)

¼ teaspoon kosher salt, plus more to taste

½ teaspoon ground white pepper

FOR THE SPICED LAMB LETTUCE CUPS

1 tablespoon extra-virgin oil

1½ pounds ground lamb or beef

2 garlic cloves, minced

1½ teaspoons kosher salt

½ teaspoon freshly ground black pepper

1 teaspoon ground coriander

½ teaspoon ground cumin

2 teaspoons Aleppo pepper (see note)

1 teaspoon toasted white sesame seeds

¼ teaspoon ground cinnamon

¼ cup low-sodium beef or chicken broth

1 head radicchio or butter lettuce, separated into individual lettuce leaves, rinsed and patted dry

Fresh mint leaves or dill fronds, for serving

In this recipe, ground lamb is cooked with a blend of delicious Mediterranean spices and served in lettuce wraps with a cooling dollop of tzatziki for a lightning-fast weeknight dinner. While the lettuce leaves offer a light, fresh alternative to pita or flatbread, you could certainly opt to serve it that way, too! You can also easily swap in ground beef for the lamb, but the depth of flavor in the lamb really makes this a one-of-a-kind easy dinner that's impressive enough to serve on the menu of a last-minute dinner party.

MAKE THE TZATZIKI: In a medium bowl, combine all the ingredients and stir until well combined. Set aside until ready to serve or you can refrigerate and use within 5 to 7 days.

MAKE THE SPICED LAMB: In a large skillet, heat the oil over medium-high heat. Add the lamb, garlic, salt, and pepper and cook, breaking up the meat into smaller pieces with a wooden spoon, until it is cooked through and no longer pink, 5 to 7 minutes. Drain off any excess fat and return the meat to the skillet.

REDUCE the heat to medium and add the coriander, cumin, Aleppo pepper, sesame seeds, and cinnamon. Cook, stirring often, until the spices are fragrant, about 2 minutes. Add the broth and cook, stirring often, until well combined with the meat and slightly reduced, about 2 minutes. Remove from the heat.

TO assemble the cups, place a spoonful of the lamb on a lettuce leaf and top with a dollop of the tzatziki. Garnish with fresh mint leaves or dill fronds.

FROM MY KITCHEN TO YOURS

Named after the northern Syrian city of Aleppo, Aleppo pepper is a mild, deep-red chile flake that is popular in Middle Eastern cuisine. If you can't find it at your local grocery store, check at a Middle Eastern grocery store or buy it on Amazon. In a pinch, sub 2 teaspoons paprika and ½ teaspoon cayenne!

Texas Tamale Pie

MAKES 4 SERVINGS • TOTAL TIME: 45 MINUTES

Growing up in the small town of Celina, Texas, I had quite the experience with casseroles—and I loved every single one. This casserole is a Texas staple called the Texas Tamale Pie. Typically it's made with ground beef cooked in enchilada sauce and topped with boxed corn bread mix, grated cheddar, and jalapeños for a little kick. It's nowhere near close to a tamale . . . but it's a fun Texas casserole dish that's just plain delicious. Here's my own paleo rendition. I love every bit of this comforting dish!

FOR THE "CORN BREAD" CRUST

2 tablespoons unsalted butter or ghee, melted and cooled (sub vegan butter for dairy-free)

2 large eggs

½ cup dairy-free creamer

1 cup almond flour

⅓ cup cassava flour

2 teaspoons baking powder

½ teaspoon paprika

¼ teaspoon kosher salt

FOR THE "TAMALE" FILLING

3 tablespoons extra-virgin olive oil

¾ cup minced yellow onion (about 1 small onion)

1½ pounds ground beef

1 teaspoon kosher salt

½ teaspoon freshly ground black pepper

1 tablespoon chili powder

1 teaspoon garlic powder

½ teaspoon ground cumin

½ teaspoon dried oregano

¼ teaspoon cayenne pepper

2 tablespoons tomato paste

One 4-ounce can diced mild green chiles

1 cup low-sodium beef broth

½ jalapeño, thinly sliced

PREHEAT the oven to 375°F.

MAKE THE "CORN BREAD" CRUST: In a large bowl, whisk the melted butter, eggs, and dairy-free creamer until pale yellow and well combined. Add the almond flour, cassava flour, baking powder, paprika, and salt and mix until well combined. Set aside.

MAKE THE "TAMALE" FILLING: In a 10-inch ovenproof skillet (preferably cast iron), heat 2 tablespoons of the olive oil over medium-high heat. Add the onion, beef, salt, and pepper and cook, breaking up the meat with a wooden spoon, until browned and cooked through, 5 to 7 minutes.

DRAIN off any excess fat and return the browned meat to the skillet. Add the chili powder, garlic powder, cumin, oregano, and cayenne and toss with the beef until well combined. Continue to cook, stirring often, to let the spices toast, about 2 minutes.

ADD the tomato paste, green chiles, and beef broth and stir to combine. Cook, scraping up the browned bits, until the meat mixture is well combined and the sauce has slightly thickened, about 3 minutes. Remove from the heat.

TO assemble, spoon the "corn bread" mixture in dollops over the meat mixture, working from the center out to the edges. Using a butter knife, evenly spread the mixture over the top as best as you can (it does not need to be perfect). Top with jalapeño slices and drizzle with the remaining 1 tablespoon olive oil.

BAKE until the crust is golden and the meat mixture is bubbling, 15 to 17 minutes. Let rest for at least 10 minutes before scooping and serving.

Fried Mortadella Sandwiches

MAKES 4 SERVINGS • TOTAL TIME: 20 MINUTES

While this meal has very minimal nutritional value, I just couldn't leave it out of this book! This is similar to a fried bologna sandwich, but my Italian heritage kicked in and I made a fried mortadella sandwich instead. It's one of those fantastic late-night dinners that you make when you really don't want to think about cooking and just want something a little greasy and a lot delicious. Pair this with some salty, crunchy potato chips and a cold Italian beer or martini. Life just doesn't get much better than that, folks!

FOR THE CREAMY DIJON SPREAD

¼ cup Homemade Mayo (page 251)

¼ cup grainy Dijon mustard

1 tablespoon brine from a jar of pepperoncini

Pinch of kosher salt

Pinch of freshly ground black pepper

FOR THE SANDWICHES

4 brioche buns, split in half horizontally

¾ pound thinly sliced mortadella (with pistachios)

8 slices provolone cheese

½ cup sliced pepperoncini

MAKE THE CREAMY DIJON SPREAD: In a small bowl or jar, combine the mayo, mustard, pepperoncini brine, salt, and pepper and stir until well combined. (This keeps well in the refrigerator for 5 to 7 days.)

MAKE THE SANDWICHES: Trim the edges of the brioche buns to form slightly smaller square buns (I find there is too much bread otherwise). Smear the insides of both sides of the buns with the creamy Dijon spread.

YOU'LL be making one sandwich at a time. Heat a large skillet, preferably cast-iron, over medium-high heat. When hot, add a bun, cut sides down, and sear until golden brown, 1 to 2 minutes. Transfer to a plate and set aside.

QUARTER-FOLD 3 or 4 slices of the mortadella, place them in a single layer in the skillet, and cook until both sides are golden brown, 2 to 3 minutes per side. Transfer to the plate with the bun and set aside.

SET a slice of provolone on each half of the bun. Place the buns, cheese side down, back in the skillet and cook until the cheese has melted and is slightly charring on the edges, about 1 minute. Using a spatula, scrape the cheese-y buns out of the skillet and transfer to a serving plate.

STACK the mortadella on the bottom half of the bun. Add about 1 tablespoon of the sliced pepperoncini to the hot skillet and cook for about 1 minute to gently soften and warm. Place the warmed pepperoncini on top of the mortadella. Smear a bit more of the Dijon spread on the top bun and place on top of the mortadella to (finally) form a sandwich.

REPEAT to make the rest of the sandwiches.

Mexican Pizza

MAKES 2 SERVINGS • TOTAL TIME: 30 MINUTES

If you were like me and grew up eating Taco Bell, you'll recognize this as the old order #4 on the menu—it was recently removed! It used to be one of my go-to orders. I love how my better-for-you version of the drive-thru classic comes together in no time and is a nostalgic treat any night of the week!

FOR THE TORTILLAS

4 grain-free tortillas (I use Siete brand)

Avocado oil cooking spray

FOR THE BEEF

1 tablespoon avocado oil

½ pound ground beef

½ teaspoon kosher salt

¼ teaspoon freshly ground black pepper

FOR THE QUICK ENCHILADA SAUCE

1 tablespoon ghee or butter (sub vegan butter for dairy-free)

1 teaspoon arrowroot flour

1 teaspoon chili powder

½ teaspoon smoked paprika

½ teaspoon ground cumin

½ teaspoon garlic powder

¼ teaspoon cayenne pepper, optional

1 tablespoon tomato paste

¾ cup low-sodium beef broth

½ teaspoon kosher salt

FOR THE PIZZAS

4 tablespoons refried black beans (omit for paleo)

¼ cup shredded Mexican cheese blend (omit for paleo and dairy-free)

FOR SERVING

1 Roma (plum) tomato, seeded and minced

1 tablespoon finely chopped fresh cilantro, optional

1 green onion, green part only, thinly sliced, optional

PREHEAT the oven to 400°F. Line a large sheet pan with parchment paper.

CRISP THE TORTILLAS: Place the tortillas on the lined sheet pan and lightly mist with cooking spray. Bake until the edges are golden brown and the tortillas are just crisp, 6 to 8 minutes.

REMOVE the sheet pan from the oven (but keep the oven on!) and set it aside.

MEANWHILE, COOK THE BEEF: In a large skillet, heat the oil over medium-high heat. Add the beef, salt, and pepper and cook, using a wooden spoon to break up the meat, until no longer pink, 5 to 7 minutes. Using a slotted spoon, transfer the meat to a bowl and set aside, leaving any rendered fat in the skillet to make the sauce.

MAKE THE QUICK ENCHILADA SAUCE: In the same skillet, melt the ghee over low heat. Add the arrowroot flour and whisk until there are no clumps. Add the chili powder, smoked paprika, cumin, garlic powder, and cayenne (if using) and cook, stirring often, until the spices are toasted and fragrant and there are no clumps, about 2 minutes. Stir in the tomato paste. While whisking, slowly add the beef broth, continuing to whisk until well combined. Add the salt, bring to a simmer, and cook until the sauce has thickened, about 2 minutes, stirring often. Remove from the heat.

ADD 2 tablespoons of the enchilada sauce to the cooked ground beef and toss to coat evenly.

ASSEMBLE THE PIZZAS: Carefully spread 2 tablespoons of the refried black beans (if using) over 2 of the crisp tortillas (still on the sheet pan). Divide the meat mixture between the bean-topped tortillas and top each with one of the remaining crisp tortillas. Divide the remaining enchilada sauce over each of the "pizzas" and gently spread to evenly coat the tops. Sprinkle each with the cheese (if using) and bake until the cheese has melted and the sauce is hot and bubbling, 2 to 3 minutes.

TO SERVE: Top with the tomato. If desired, garnish with cilantro and green onions.

Sheet Pan Kielbasa with Mustard Vinaigrette

GLUTEN-FREE (IF MODIFIED)
DAIRY-FREE
PALEO (IF MODIFIED)
WHOLE30 (IF MODIFIED)
GRAIN-FREE (IF MODIFIED)

MAKES 4 SERVINGS • TOTAL TIME: 40 MINUTES

When serving a crowd, my mother-in-law loves to make beer-braised bratwursts. They're easy to make and a total crowd-pleaser. Here I've taken those flavors and turned them into a festive sheet pan dinner complete with a mustard vinaigrette that's bursting with flavor.

FOR THE SHEET PAN

1½ pounds baby Dutch yellow potatoes, unpeeled (or regular yellow potatoes cut into 2-inch wedges)

3 tablespoons extra-virgin olive oil

½ teaspoon kosher salt, plus more to taste

½ teaspoon freshly ground black pepper

1 medium head red cabbage, cut into ½-inch-thick wedges

One 14-ounce kielbasa sausage, cut on the diagonal into 3-inch pieces

1 small yellow onion, halved and thinly sliced

¾ cup beer (sub low-sodium chicken broth for Whole30, paleo, gluten-free, grain-free)

FOR THE MUSTARD VINAIGRETTE

2 tablespoons extra-virgin olive oil

2 tablespoons white wine vinegar

1 tablespoon whole-grain mustard

2 teaspoons Dijon mustard

1 tablespoon chopped fresh dill

Pinch of kosher salt

Pinch of freshly ground black pepper

FOR SERVING

1 lemon, cut into wedges

Fresh dill fronds, for garnish

PREHEAT the oven to 400°F. Line a large rimmed sheet pan with parchment paper.

MAKE THE SHEET PAN: Place the potatoes on the lined sheet pan, drizzle with 2 tablespoons of the olive oil, and season with the salt and pepper. Toss until well combined and bake for 10 minutes.

REMOVE the sheet pan from the oven and add the red cabbage, kielbasa, and yellow onion. Drizzle with the remaining 1 tablespoon olive oil. Using a spatula, gently toss until well combined with the potatoes and evenly coated with the olive oil. Spread into a single layer and bake for another 10 minutes.

REMOVE from the oven and pour the beer over the sheet pan, coating all the ingredients in the tray. Carefully return the sheet pan to the oven and cook until the cabbage has browned and the beer has evaporated, 12 to 15 minutes.

MEANWHILE, MAKE THE MUSTARD VINAIGRETTE: In a medium bowl, combine the olive oil, vinegar, whole-grain mustard, Dijon mustard, chopped dill, salt, and pepper and whisk until well combined.

SERVE with lemon wedges, garnish with the dill fronds, and drizzle with the mustard vinaigrette.

Perfectly Broiled Rib Eye with Tarragon Butter

MAKES 4 SERVINGS • TOTAL TIME: 25 MINUTES

Making a big, juicy rib-eye steak usually has lots of opportunities for error. But not anymore! Here is a foolproof method that turns out absolutely perfect every time. All you need is a few ingredients, including good-quality rib-eye steaks. This skillet-to-oven method works like a charm! You'll feel like you're in a five-star restaurant.

FOR THE TARRAGON BUTTER

2 tablespoons salted butter, at room temperature

2 garlic cloves, minced

1 tablespoon finely chopped fresh tarragon leaves

FOR THE RIB-EYE STEAKS

2 rib-eye steaks, 1½ inches thick (about 1 pound each), at room temperature (see note)

2½ teaspoons kosher salt

1 teaspoon freshly ground black pepper

2 tablespoons avocado oil

Flaky salt, for garnish

PAIRING SUGGESTIONS: **Little Gem Salad with Lemon Dressing (page 204), Parmesan-Roasted Zucchini (page 195), Balsamic-Thyme Roasted Mushrooms (page 199)**

FROM MY KITCHEN TO YOURS

When cooking a steak, you always want to bring it to room temperature before searing. This keeps the meat from seizing when it hits a hot pan and helps the steak cook evenly. Since these are thick rib eyes, take them out of the fridge 30 minutes before cooking for a perfect result.

MAKE THE TARRAGON BUTTER: In a small bowl, combine the butter, garlic, and tarragon. Stir until well combined. Set aside.

COOK THE RIB-EYE STEAKS: Heat a cast-iron or heavy-bottomed skillet over medium-high heat until very hot but not smoking.

MEANWHILE, pat the steaks very dry. Generously season all sides of each steak with the salt and pepper, pressing in the seasoning so it adheres to the meat. Make sure to season the entire surface, including the sides and fat cap.

SET an oven rack in the highest position and turn the oven to high broil.

ADD the avocado oil to the hot skillet and swirl to coat evenly. Sear the steaks individually (so that you do not overcrowd the pan) undisturbed for about 1 minute per side, until a golden crust forms. Finally, turn the steak on its edge and sear the fat cap for about 30 seconds, just until it begins to render.

TRANSFER the steaks to a sheet pan and broil to your desired doneness. I cook mine for exactly 5 minutes for medium-rare. If your steaks are closer to 2 inches thick, cook for 1 minute more, and if they are closer to 1 inch thick, cook for 1 minute less.

CAREFULLY remove the hot sheet pan from the oven. Dividing evenly, top the steaks with the tarragon butter. Let the steaks rest on the hot pan for about 8 minutes while the butter melts.

TRANSFER the steaks to a cutting board, slice against the grain, and serve immediately. Finish with a pinch of flaky salt.

Juicy Indoor Burgers with Burger Sauce

GLUTEN-FREE (IF MODIFIED; SEE NOTE)
DAIRY-FREE (IF MODIFIED; SEE NOTE)
PALEO (IF MODIFIED; SEE NOTE)
GRAIN-FREE (IF MODIFIED; SEE NOTE)

MAKES 4 SERVINGS • TOTAL TIME: 25 MINUTES

Burgers are always a good choice—but not all burgers are created equal. It's important to pay attention to the way you cook your burger. This simple method will guarantee your "indoor burgers" (not cooked on a grill) turn out perfect every time. Taking care not to overwork the meat and seasoning the patties right before cooking is the key. The more you mess with a burger, the less tender it will be. Just let them be! Oh, and top them with this fantastic burger sauce . . . and your burger game is sure to be on point.

FOR THE BURGER SAUCE

½ cup Homemade Mayo (page 251)

¼ cup finely minced yellow onion

2 tablespoons ketchup (I use Primal Kitchen Unsweetened)

2 tablespoons coconut sugar

1 tablespoon dill relish

2 teaspoons yellow mustard

1 teaspoon white wine vinegar

¼ teaspoon kosher salt, plus more to taste

FOR THE BURGERS

1¼ pounds ground beef, at room temperature

2 tablespoons avocado oil

1½ teaspoons kosher salt

½ teaspoon freshly ground black pepper

FOR SERVING

4 slices mild cheddar cheese

4 brioche buns, split in half horizontally

2 tablespoons unsalted butter, at room temperature

Green leaf lettuce leaves

1 medium beefsteak tomato, thinly sliced

½ medium red onion, thinly sliced

PAIRING SUGGESTION: Zesty Potato Wedges (page 210)

MAKE THE BURGER SAUCE: In a small bowl, combine all the burger sauce ingredients and mix well. Refrigerate until ready to serve. (This keeps for 5 to 7 days in the refrigerator.)

MAKE THE BURGERS: Evenly divide the ground beef into 4 portions. Without overworking the meat, form thin patties about 5 inches wide and ¼ inch thick. If they are too thick, they will seize up in the pan. Set aside.

HEAT a large cast-iron skillet over medium-high heat until the skillet is very hot but not smoking, about 5 minutes. Add the avocado oil.

IMMEDIATELY before placing the burgers in the skillet, generously season both sides of the patties with the salt and black pepper. Gently place the patties in the hot skillet and cook until the burgers have formed a deep-brown crust on both sides and are cooked to your liking, 2 to 3 minutes per side for medium-rare. Transfer the cooked patties to a plate and let rest. If you are using cheese, place a slice of cheddar on top of each burger while they rest to melt a bit.

TOAST THE BUNS: Reduce the heat in the skillet to medium heat. Smear about ½ tablespoon butter on the insides of the buns and toast butter side down until golden brown, 2 to 3 minutes.

TO SERVE: Spread your desired amount of burger sauce on the inside of each bun. Add the burger patty and load the burger up with the toppings you desire. I add lettuce, tomato, and onion to mine for a classic burger, but you can get as fancy as you want!

FROM MY KITCHEN TO YOURS

To modify this dish to be gluten-free, dairy-free, paleo, and grain-free, omit the cheese and serve in butter lettuce leaves instead of the bun!

Green Chile Pork Medallions

MAKES 4 SERVINGS • TOTAL TIME: 55 MINUTES

GLUTEN-FREE
DAIRY-FREE (IF MODIFIED)
WHOLE30 (IF MODIFIED)
PALEO (IF MODIFIED)
GRAIN-FREE

1½ pounds red potatoes, unpeeled, cut into 2-inch cubes

1 teaspoon kosher salt

FOR THE PORK

2 pounds pork tenderloin

2 teaspoons kosher salt

1 teaspoon freshly ground black pepper

¼ cup cassava flour

4 tablespoons extra-virgin olive oil

FOR THE HATCH CHILE GRAVY

2 tablespoons unsalted butter (sub ghee for paleo and Whole30, and vegan butter for dairy-free)

2 garlic cloves, minced

¼ cup dry white wine (sub low-sodium chicken broth for paleo and Whole30)

½ cup chopped roasted Hatch green chiles from a jar (see note)

½ cup low-sodium chicken broth

½ teaspoon ground cumin

½ teaspoon dried oregano

FOR THE MASHED POTATOES

2 tablespoons unsalted butter (sub ghee for paleo and Whole30, and vegan butter for dairy-free)

2 garlic cloves, minced

½ cup low-sodium chicken broth

¼ cup dairy-free creamer or unsweetened, full-fat coconut milk

1 teaspoon kosher salt

½ teaspoon freshly ground black pepper

2 tablespoons chopped fresh cilantro, for serving

If you aren't familiar with the magic of Hatch green chiles, it's time to change that. The popular New Mexico chile has its own unique flavor that creates a lot of buzz in the South, especially when it is in season in the late summer. The chiles can be spicy or mild (depending on the batch) but they always have a beautiful, earthy, and smoky flavor. While finding fresh Hatch chiles is awesome, a ton of brands roast them, chop them, and sell them in a jar or can. That way, you can enjoy Hatch chiles year-round and add incredible flavor to any dish! This easy skillet pork dish is insanely delicious and the perfect way to enjoy Hatch chiles any day of the week!

IN a medium saucepan, combine the potatoes with water to cover by about 2 inches. Bring the water to a boil over medium-high heat. Add the salt and boil until the potatoes are fork-tender, 12 to 14 minutes. Drain off the water and set the potatoes and saucepan aside until you are ready to make the mash.

MAKE THE PORK: Trim the pork of the silver skin and slice the tenderloin crosswise into 1-inch-thick rounds. Place the pork slices on a cutting board and cover with parchment paper. Using a meat mallet or the back of a skillet, pound the pork rounds to a ¼-inch thickness.

SEASON both sides of the pork with the salt and pepper. Spread the cassava flour on a large plate. Dredge each pork medallion in cassava flour on both sides and shake off the excess.

IN a large deep skillet, heat 2 tablespoons of the olive oil over medium-high heat. Working in two batches, carefully place the pork medallions in the oil, taking care not to overcrowd the pan. This will ensure that they brown nicely. Sear until each side is golden brown, about 2 minutes per side. Repeat with the remaining pork and 2 tablespoons oil for the second batch. Transfer the medallions to a plate and set aside (they do not need to be fully cooked at this point).

MAKE THE HATCH CHILE GRAVY: Reduce the heat to medium under the skillet. Add the butter and garlic and cook, stirring and taking care not to burn the garlic, about 1 minute. Add the wine and continue to cook, stirring often and scraping up any browned bits, to deglaze the pan, until the wine has reduced by half.

FROM MY KITCHEN TO YOURS

Hatch green chiles can pack a punch! I use medium-heat chiles. If you'd like less heat, definitely go with the mild chiles!

ADD the green chiles, chicken broth, cumin, and oregano and cook, stirring often, until the sauce is simmering. Reduce the heat to medium-low so that the sauce is only lightly simmering and nestle the browned pork medallions into it (it's okay if they're a little crowded). Cook, uncovered, until the pork is tender and the sauce has thickened, about 10 minutes.

MEANWHILE, MAKE THE MASHED POTATOES: Heat the (empty) saucepan you used to boil the potatoes over medium heat and melt the butter. Add the garlic and sauté for 1 minute. Reduce the heat to low and add the boiled potatoes. Using a potato masher, mash the potatoes until almost smooth. Add the broth, creamer, salt, and pepper. Continue to mash until the potatoes reach your desired consistency. Cover and remove from the heat.

TO SERVE: Divide the mashed potatoes among four plates and top with the pork medallions, chile gravy, and cilantro. Enjoy!

Tender Oven-Baked Ribs with Vinegary BBQ Sauce

GLUTEN-FREE
DAIRY-FREE
PALEO
GRAIN-FREE

MAKES 4 SERVINGS • TOTAL TIME: 2 HOURS 30 MINUTES

FOR THE RIBS

3 pounds baby back pork ribs (see note)

1 tablespoon avocado oil

1½ teaspoons kosher salt

1 tablespoon freshly ground black pepper

1½ teaspoons smoked paprika

½ teaspoon garlic powder

FOR THE VINEGARY BBQ SAUCE

1 cup unsweetened ketchup (I use Primal Kitchen)

1 cup apple cider vinegar

1 teaspoon smoked paprika

½ teaspoon cayenne pepper, optional

½ teaspoon garlic powder

1 tablespoon coconut aminos

1 tablespoon coconut sugar

1 teaspoon kosher salt

1 teaspoon freshly ground black pepper

PAIRING SUGGESTION: Braised Brussels Sprouts (page 208)

FROM MY KITCHEN TO YOURS

CHOOSING RIBS: Racks of ribs come in varying sizes and weights; sometimes I'll need two racks and other times one rack is plenty. Just be sure it's about 3 pounds total.

STORING THE SAUCE: Leftover vinegary BBQ sauce will keep up to 1 month in the refrigerator.

In Texas, barbecue is a way of life; while many of my fellow Texans will turn their nose up at the fact that I oven-roast these ribs, they'll get over it! Life is too short to huff and puff when there are ribs to be eaten. The vinegary BBQ sauce makes these simply irresistible—so tangy, a little spicy, and just straight-up delicious. So fire up your smokers . . . er, ovens . . . and get to eating some ribs, y'all!

PREHEAT the oven to 275°F. Line a large sheet pan with foil.

PREPARE THE RIBS: If the ribs still have the thin membrane covering the back of the rack, remove it; it can become tough when cooked. To do this, place the ribs meaty side down on a cutting board. Carefully and gently slide a paring knife under a corner of the membrane to loosen and lift the corner from the rack of the ribs. Using your fingers, pull the membrane away from the bones. If it's slippery or difficult to remove, use a kitchen towel to get a better grip on the ribs.

PLACE the ribs on the lined sheet pan and pat them dry on both sides with paper towels. Set them meaty side up on the pan and drizzle with the avocado oil to evenly coat the top of the ribs.

IN a small bowl, combine the salt, pepper, smoked paprika, and garlic powder. Evenly season both sides of the ribs with the spice mixture.

COVER the sheet pan very tightly with another piece of foil. Bake for 2 hours. The ribs should be cooked through and tender, but not quite fall-off-the-bone so that they hold their shape.

MEANWHILE, MAKE THE VINEGARY BBQ SAUCE: In a small saucepan, combine all the ingredients and bring to a light simmer over medium heat. Cook, stirring often, so there are no lumps and the sauce has just thickened, about 5 minutes. Set aside to cool.

FINISH THE RIBS: Remove the ribs from the oven and increase the temperature to 325°F. Uncover them and brush the tops generously with ⅓ cup of the BBQ sauce. Return the ribs to the oven, uncovered, and bake for 15 minutes. Remove the ribs from the oven and coat again with ⅓ cup BBQ sauce.

SET the oven to broil and broil until a deep crust begins to form and the sauce begins to caramelize on the top of the ribs, 3 to 4 minutes.

SERVE with the remaining BBQ sauce.

Italian Braciole

MAKES 6 SERVINGS • TOTAL TIME: 1 HOUR 25 MINUTES

If you grew up in an Italian family, you've probably had braciole as a signature dish around the holidays or for special occasions. This is a bit of a project to tackle on a Sunday, but I promise the end product is totally worth the effort. The traditional version is either flank steak or round steak, pounded thin, stuffed with a bread crumb and egg mixture, covered with marinara and cheese, and cooked until the meat is tender and the cheese is bubbling. My version is updated with fresh herbs and a good jarred marinara to cut down on your hands-on time. This is sure to be a showstopper on your table, whether it's a holiday or just your average Sunday!

FOR THE FILLING

⅔ cup freshly shredded Parmesan cheese

⅓ cup plain gluten-free bread crumbs

⅓ cup finely chopped fresh parsley

3 garlic cloves, minced

½ teaspoon crushed red pepper flakes, optional

¼ cup extra-virgin olive oil

FOR THE BRACIOLE

1½ pounds top sirloin steak

1 teaspoon kosher salt

½ teaspoon freshly ground black pepper

6 slices prosciutto

2 tablespoons extra-virgin olive oil

One 24-ounce jar marinara sauce (I like Rao's brand)

¼ cup freshly shredded Parmesan cheese

2 tablespoons chopped fresh parsley

SPECIAL EQUIPMENT

Kitchen twine or toothpicks, for securing the rolls

PAIRING SUGGESTIONS: **Little Gem Salad with Lemon Dressing (page 204), Parmesan-Roasted Zucchini (page 195)**

PREHEAT the oven to 325°F.

MAKE THE FILLING: In a medium bowl, combine the Parmesan, bread crumbs, parsley, garlic, pepper flakes, and olive oil and stir until well mixed. Set aside.

MAKE THE BRACIOLE: Trim any excess fat off the sirloin. Using a very sharp knife, cut the sirloin in half, then slice each half into 3 filets, to give you 6 filets of equal size. Place the filets on a cutting board, lay a sheet of parchment paper over each filet, and use a meat mallet or the bottom of a heavy skillet to pound it to an even ¼-inch thickness. Remove the parchment paper and lightly season both sides of the filets with the salt and pepper.

PLACE a slice of prosciutto on top of each filet, then evenly divide the Parmesan filling over the prosciutto. Spread it so that it evenly coats each slice of prosciutto.

CAREFULLY roll up each piece to make a roulade. Flip the roulade so it is seam side up and truss it with kitchen twine or close it up with a toothpick. Continue to make all 6 rolls.

IN a large skillet, heat the olive oil over medium-high heat until the oil is shimmering. In batches, carefully transfer the beef to the skillet and sear on all sides until a golden-brown crust forms, 2 to 3 minutes per side, 8 to 12 minutes total.

TRANSFER the browned roulades and their juices to a 2½-quart oval baking dish or 9 × 13-inch baking dish. Arrange them in a single layer across the dish. Pour the marinara over the beef, making sure each roulade is covered. Cover the dish tightly with foil and bake until the beef is very tender, about 45 minutes.

CAREFULLY remove the foil. Remove the kitchen twine or toothpick from each roulade. Sprinkle with the Parmesan and parsley and let cool for 5 minutes before serving.

Texas-Style Instant Pot or Slow Cooker Brisket Tacos

MAKES 8 SERVINGS • TOTAL TIME: 1 HOUR 45 MINUTES OR 6 TO 8 HOURS

Texas has given me so many things in life that I'm grateful for, and brisket tacos are at the top of the list. If you've never visited Dallas, I encourage you to hop on the next flight and head straight to Mia's Tex-Mex for their brisket tacos. Holy yum! Mia's is a Dallas fixture and arguably the best in town across the board, but it's especially known for these tacos. The best part? The side of brisket gravy served in the center of the plate for dipping. Whoa. Here's my rendition of them, which can be made in either a slow cooker or an Instant Pot.

FOR THE SAUCE

2 tablespoons tomato paste

2 teaspoons Dijon mustard

¼ cup coconut aminos

¼ cup low-sodium beef broth

½ teaspoon chipotle chile powder

½ teaspoon ground cumin

FOR THE BRISKET

3 pounds flat-cut brisket

2 teaspoons kosher salt

1 teaspoon freshly ground black pepper

2 tablespoons extra-virgin olive oil

FOR THE TACOS

1 tablespoon extra-virgin olive oil

2 medium poblano peppers, halved, seeded, and thinly sliced

1 medium white onion, halved and thinly sliced

16 grain-free tortillas (I use Siete brand; sub lettuce cups for Whole30)

2 tablespoons chopped fresh cilantro, for serving

2 limes, cut into wedges, for serving

PAIRING SUGGESTION: Clayton's Margarita (page 230)

INSTANT POT METHOD

MAKE THE SAUCE: In a bowl, whisk all of the sauce ingredients together to combine. Set aside.

PREPARE THE BRISKET: Trim the excess fat from the brisket and cut the meat into 3 even pieces. Pat very dry with paper towels. Season with the salt and pepper on all sides, pressing into the meat to coat.

SET the Instant Pot to the "sauté" function. When hot, add the olive oil. Working in batches to avoid overcrowding, sear the brisket until a golden-brown crust has formed on all sides, about 3 minutes per side. Transfer the browned brisket to a plate as you work.

TURN off the Instant Pot. Pour the sauce into the Instant Pot and nestle the brisket pieces into the liquid. Lock the lid, making sure the vent is sealed. Press the "manual" or "pressure cook" button (depending on your model) and set the time to 60 minutes. Walk away from the Instant Pot and let it do its thing!

WHEN the cook time is complete, release the pressure manually by carefully turning the valve to venting. When all the pressure has been released, carefully remove the lid and transfer the brisket to a rimmed sheet pan. Do not discard the liquid in the Instant Pot.

USING two forks, shred the brisket. Ladle about ¾ cup of the liquid in the Instant Pot over the meat and toss to coat. The brisket will start to absorb the liquid. Add ¾ cup more of the liquid to the meat and toss to coat.

SET the Instant Pot to the "sauté" function and bring the liquid remaining in the Instant Pot to a rapid boil. Cook, whisking occasionally, until the gravy thickens and reduces, 8 to 10 minutes. Remove from the heat and let cool for an additional 8 to 10 minutes.

(recipe continues)

Broccoli Casserole

1 pkg. chopped broccoli (frozen)
1 small jar cheese whiz (or ½ jar)
1 cup cooked rice
1 can mushroom soup
½ cup chopped onion
½ cup chopped celery

Mix all together. Bake at
350° until it bubbles

Italia[n]

1 lb. rnd. steak (
1 pkg. (5 oz) nood[le]
1 can tomato so[up]
¼ lb. bacon
1 med. grn. pepp[er]
2 T. worchestershi[re]
2 med. onions (c[ut])
1 sm. can pimien[to]
¼ lb. sharp chee[se]

CREATIVE TAMALE PIE

1½ POUNDS GROUND BEEF
½ ONION, CHOPPED
2 CLOVES GARLIC, MINCED
1 LARGE CAN CORN, DRAINED
2 CUPS TOMATO SAUCE (OR 15 OZ. CAN)
1 TABLESPOON CHILI POWDER
1 TEASPOON SALT
1 CUP BLACK PITTED OLIVES
2 EGGS
1 CUP MILK
1 CUP YELLOW CORN MEAL

(OVER)

Spoonburgers

[grou]nd beef
[tablesp]oons fat
[ch]opped onion
[spoo]n prepared mustard
[spoo]n catsup

½ TEASPOON SALT
⅛ TEASPOON
1 10½
s[oup]

[Coo]k in hot fat; ad[d]
[ ] remaining ingre[dients]
[ ] minutes. Spoon from o[ven]

Pea Salad

1 can peas (drained)
1 can green beans (drai[ned])
2 cups chopped cel[ery]
1 large onion
[ ] pimien[to]

DEFROST IF FROZE[N]
MARINATE IF FROZ[EN]
LOW FOR [ ]

Chicken in Barbe[cue]

1 cup flour
1 teaspoon salt
¼ teaspoon pepper
1 (3 lb.)

PACKA[GE]
COO[K]
CUPS
LARG[E]
GRATE[D]
¾ CUPS
½ CUP
1 TEASP[OON]
½ TEASPO[ON]
½ TEASP[OON]
1 TEASP[OON]
EGGS
UP
SI[ ]

MEANWHILE, FOR THE TACOS: In a large skillet (preferably cast iron), heat the olive oil over medium-high heat. Add the poblano peppers and onion and sauté, tossing occasionally, until the vegetables are slightly tender, about 7 minutes.

PLACE the tortillas, one at a time, in a dry (no oil) stainless steel skillet over medium heat and cook for about 30 seconds per side. You can also do away with the skillet and char the tortillas directly over a gas flame for a few seconds using tongs.

TO assemble the tacos, fill the warmed tortillas with the brisket, poblano peppers, and onions. Top with cilantro and serve with a side of the gravy and lime wedges.

SLOW COOKER METHOD

MAKE THE SAUCE: In a bowl, combine all of the sauce ingredients and whisk to combine. Set aside.

PREPARE THE BRISKET: Trim the excess fat from the brisket and cut the meat into 3 even pieces. Pat them very dry with paper towels. Season with the salt and pepper on all sides, pressing into the meat to coat.

IN a large skillet, heat the oil over medium-high heat. Working in batches so as not to overcrowd the pan, sear the brisket until a golden-brown crust has formed on all sides, about 3 minutes per side.

POUR the sauce into the slow cooker and nestle the browned brisket inside. Set the slow cooker to low, cover, and cook for 6 to 8 hours, until the brisket is tender and shreds easily with a fork.

WHEN the cook time is complete, remove the lid and transfer the brisket to a rimmed sheet pan (do not discard the liquid in the slow cooker).

USING two forks, shred the brisket. Ladle about ¾ cup of the liquid in the slow cooker over the meat and toss to coat. The brisket will start to absorb the liquid. Add ¾ cup more of the liquid to the meat and toss to coat.

TRANSFER the remaining liquid from the slow cooker to a small saucepan. Bring the liquid to a rapid simmer. Cook, whisking occasionally, until the gravy thickens and reduces, 8 to 10 minutes. Remove from the heat and let cool for an additional 8 to 10 minutes.

CONTINUE as above with "for the tacos."

chicken

Crispy Chicken Milanese with Arugula Salad

MAKES 4 SERVINGS • TOTAL TIME: 30 MINUTES

FOR THE CHICKEN MILANESE

2 boneless, skinless chicken breasts

1 teaspoon kosher salt

½ teaspoon freshly ground black pepper

1 large egg

2 teaspoons Dijon mustard

1 cup gluten-free panko bread crumbs

2 tablespoons extra-virgin olive oil

FOR THE ARUGULA-TOMATO SALAD

4 cups baby arugula

1 cup halved grape tomatoes

¼ cup shaved Parmesan cheese (omit for dairy-free)

1 tablespoon extra-virgin olive oil

1 tablespoon freshly squeezed lemon juice (about ½ lemon)

½ lemon, cut into wedges, for serving

Milanese is an Italian dish that's traditionally prepared with veal and made into a breaded cutlet, fried in butter or oil; chicken Milanese is a popular variation of the dish in the United States. When Clayton and I first started dating, I made it for him often, and it's still one of my favorite meals—I mean, there aren't really many folks who don't love a crispy breaded chicken cutlet, especially when it's topped with a lemony arugula salad. My kiddos love this dish (minus the arugula salad part), and it's a weeknight go-to for sure!

PREPARE THE CHICKEN MILANESE: Place the chicken breasts on a cutting board and cut them in half horizontally. Cover with parchment paper or plastic wrap and use a meat mallet or the bottom of a heavy skillet to pound the chicken to a uniform ¼-inch thickness. Pat dry with a paper towel, season both sides of the chicken with the salt and pepper, and set aside.

IN a large, shallow bowl, whisk the egg and mustard until well combined. Pour the panko into a separate large, shallow bowl. Set the bowls next to each other for dredging.

IN a large nonstick skillet, heat the oil over medium heat until shimmering.

DIP a piece of chicken first in the egg mixture and shake off the excess. Then, dredge the chicken in the panko, pressing it into the chicken to help it adhere. Carefully lay the chicken into the oil and fry until golden brown on both sides and cooked through, about 3 minutes per side. Transfer the cooked chicken to a plate lined with paper towels and repeat with the remaining pieces of chicken.

MAKE THE ARUGULA-TOMATO SALAD: In a large bowl, combine the arugula, tomatoes, Parmesan (if using), olive oil, and lemon juice and toss to combine.

DIVIDE the chicken among four plates and top with the arugula-tomato salad. Serve with lemon wedges.

Ultimate Skillet Chicken Fajitas

MAKES 6 SERVINGS • TOTAL TIME: 1 HOUR 10 MINUTES

FOR THE CHICKEN

¼ cup avocado oil

¼ cup freshly squeezed lime juice (about 2 limes)

2 teaspoons kosher salt

1 teaspoon freshly ground black pepper

2 teaspoons dried oregano

1 teaspoon chili powder

1 teaspoon ground cumin

1 teaspoon smoked paprika

2½ pounds boneless, skinless chicken thighs, trimmed of excess fat

FOR THE VEGETABLES

1 green bell pepper, sliced into ¼-inch-wide strips

1 red bell pepper, sliced into ¼-inch-wide strips

1 medium white onion, halved and cut into ¼-inch-thick slices

1 tablespoon freshly squeezed lime juice (about ½ lime)

1 tablespoon avocado oil

FOR THE GARLIC-HERB BUTTER

3 tablespoons salted butter (sub ghee for Whole30 and paleo; sub vegan butter for dairy-free)

3 garlic cloves, minced

¼ to ½ teaspoon crushed red pepper flakes, to taste

1 tablespoon finely chopped fresh oregano

PAIRING SUGGESTIONS: **Brothy Borracho Beans (page 203), Mezcal Mule (page 234)**

There's something about getting fajitas at a restaurant that just feels like a celebration. They come to the table still sizzling and are always a treat. Luckily, they're just as easy to make at home! The marinade for this chicken packs a ton of Tex-Mex flavor, and the garlic-herb butter just sends it over the top.

PREPARE THE CHICKEN: In a large bowl, whisk together the avocado oil, lime juice, salt, pepper, dried oregano, chili powder, cumin, and smoked paprika. Add the chicken and toss until evenly coated. Set aside and let the chicken marinate at room temperature for about 20 minutes. (Alternatively, cover the bowl with plastic wrap and transfer to the fridge to marinate for up to 24 hours.)

HEAT a large cast-iron skillet over medium-high heat. When the skillet is very hot, add the chicken, taking care not to overcrowd the pan. You'll likely have to do this in multiple batches. Sear the chicken on both sides until golden brown, 3 to 4 minutes per side. Transfer the cooked chicken to a cutting board and set aside to rest.

COOK THE VEGGIES: In the same skillet, combine both bell peppers, the onion, and lime juice. Toss to soak up any remaining juices in the skillet, scraping up the browned bits. Add the avocado oil and cook, tossing occasionally, until the veggies are tender, about 5 minutes.

MAKE THE GARLIC-HERB BUTTER: Heat a small saucepan over medium-low heat. Add the butter, garlic, pepper flakes, and fresh oregano. Melt the butter and cook, stirring often and taking care not to burn the butter, until the flavors have just combined, 2 to 3 minutes.

TO SERVE: Spread the veggies across a large serving platter. Slice the chicken into strips about ¼ inch thick and place on top of the veggies, along with any juices. Spoon the garlic-herb butter over the top.

GLUTEN-FREE
DAIRY-FREE
PALEO
WHOLE30
GRAIN-FREE

Dilly Chicken Burgers with Spicy Slaw

MAKES 6 SERVINGS • TOTAL TIME: 30 MINUTES

One of my favorite combinations in life is something really spicy with a dill pickle on the side or on it . . . dill pickles + spicy stuff = love. Inspired by a spicy hot chicken sandwich, I've made a very simple yet ultra dilly and juicy chicken burger patty and topped it off with a hot and spicy slaw. The end result is delightful if you're like me and love that combo! If you're not like me and don't like things spicy, you can top these delicious burgers with a classic slaw instead, or just serve them on a bun and call it a day. Whatever your heart desires is good with me!

FOR THE SPICY SLAW

2 tablespoons Homemade Mayo (page 251)

2 tablespoons Louisiana-style hot sauce (I use Crystal)

1 teaspoon spicy brown mustard

1 teaspoon paprika

½ teaspoon chili powder

½ teaspoon garlic powder

¼ teaspoon cayenne pepper

One 12-ounce bag coleslaw mix or finely shredded cabbage (about 4 cups)

Kosher salt and freshly ground black pepper, to taste

FOR THE DILLY CHICKEN BURGERS

1½ pounds ground chicken breast

2 tablespoons Homemade Mayo (page 251)

¼ cup minced dill pickle or dill relish

¼ cup finely minced fresh dill

2 garlic cloves, minced

1 tablespoon freshly squeezed lemon juice (about ½ lemon)

1 teaspoon onion powder

1 teaspoon kosher salt

½ teaspoon freshly ground black pepper

¼ cup tapioca or arrowroot flour

2 tablespoons avocado oil

OPTIONAL FOR SERVING

1 head butter lettuce

Sliced dill pickles

PAIRING SUGGESTION: **Zesty Potato Wedges (page 210)**

MAKE THE SPICY SLAW: In a large bowl, combine the mayo, hot sauce, mustard, paprika, chili powder, garlic powder, and cayenne pepper and whisk until well combined. Add the coleslaw mix and toss until very well combined. Add salt and pepper to taste and set aside.

MAKE THE BURGERS: In a separate large bowl, combine the ground chicken, mayo, dill pickle, fresh dill, garlic, lemon juice, onion powder, salt, pepper, and tapioca flour. Mix until very well combined.

FORM the chicken mixture into 6 equal burger patties. (Damp hands help if you are having difficulty forming the patties.)

IN a large skillet (preferably cast iron), heat the avocado oil over medium-high heat until shimmering.

CAREFULLY place the patties in the oil, working in batches as needed, and cook until golden brown on both sides and the chicken is cooked through and no longer pink, 3 to 4 minutes per side.

SERVE each burger patty topped with the spicy slaw. If desired, place the patties on a few pieces of butter lettuce and serve with sliced pickles.

Paleo Pot Pies

MAKES 4 SERVINGS • TOTAL TIME: 1 HOUR

GLUTEN-FREE
DAIRY-FREE (IF MODIFIED)
GRAIN-FREE
PALEO

FOR THE PIE CRUST

1 cup super-fine almond flour

⅓ cup arrowroot flour

½ teaspoon kosher salt

¼ teaspoon baking powder

¼ cup ghee or unsalted butter, chilled in the refrigerator or freezer until solid (sub vegan butter for dairy-free)

1 large egg, whisked

1 tablespoon ice cold water, plus more as needed

FOR THE FILLING

2 tablespoons ghee or unsalted butter (sub vegan butter for dairy-free)

½ cup minced yellow onion (about ½ small onion)

½ cup minced celery

½ cup minced carrot

2 garlic cloves, minced

1 teaspoon kosher salt

½ teaspoon freshly ground black pepper

1 teaspoon finely chopped fresh thyme leaves, plus more for serving

2 tablespoons arrowroot flour

1 cup low-sodium chicken broth

½ cup dairy-free creamer (sub heavy cream if not dairy-free)

2 cups diced cooked chicken (store-bought rotisserie or Fauxtisserie Chicken, page 247)

½ cup frozen peas

Grated zest of ½ lemon, optional

Dash of cayenne pepper, optional

FOR THE TOPPING

1 large egg, whisked

Flaky salt, optional for topping

There's really nothing quite as comforting as a hot, bubbling chicken pot pie. Not to call out my own mother, but we grew up on the store-bought freezer version of chicken pot pie, and we absolutely loved when we had it for dinner. Well, this recipe is much better tasting than the freezer ones my mom popped into the oven and is packed with wholesome ingredients. I'll admit that this is definitely the most cumbersome recipe in the book, but the end result is worth it if you are craving a comforting chicken pot pie. The rich, savory filling is just bursting with flavor, and that crisp, buttery crust is pure heaven.

PREHEAT the oven to 400°F.

MAKE THE PIE CRUST: In a food processor, combine the almond flour, arrowroot flour, salt, and baking powder. Process until well combined and lump free.

PLACE the ghee (or butter) on a cutting board. Cut it into ½-inch cubes and add to the food processor. Pulse until the ghee is broken apart into the flour mixture and you have an even and crumbly consistency. You want small pieces of ghee about the size of peas.

ADD the egg and pulse 5 or 6 times, until the dough starts to come together. Take a bit of the dough into your palm. If you can press the dough together into a ball, no need to add water. Is your mix a bit too dry and crumbly? Add 1 tablespoon of cold water at a time and pulse until you can press the dough together into a ball.

TRANSFER the dough to a 12-inch-long sheet of parchment paper. Place another 12-inch-long sheet of parchment paper on top and use a rolling pin or your hands to smooth out the dough into an even, thin layer, about ¼ inch thick and large enough to cover the tops of four 6-ounce ramekins.

TRANSFER the dough to the fridge and chill while you prepare the filling.

MAKE THE FILLING: In a large deep skillet, heat the ghee over medium heat. Add the onion, celery, carrot, garlic, salt, pepper, and thyme and cook, stirring often, until the veggies are tender, 5 to 7 minutes.

SPRINKLE in the arrowroot flour and stir it into the veggies until well combined. Stirring constantly, slowly pour the chicken broth into the skillet until it is well incorporated. Continuing to stir, do the same with the creamer. Simmer, stirring constantly, until the sauce is thick and creamy, 4 to 5 minutes. Remove from the heat and stir in the diced chicken, frozen peas, lemon zest (if using), and cayenne (if using).

ASSEMBLE THE POT PIES: Place four 6-ounce ramekins on a sheet pan and evenly divide the filling among them. The sheet pan saves you from any drippage in the oven.

NOW, here is the tricky part—but trust me, even if you mess up the crust, you can rebuild it on each of the ramekins and it will turn out perfect. *Okay? Cool.* This crust is *not* easy to work with. It's a little softer than the dough you might be used to, but it tastes absolutely fantastic when it is done.

REMOVE the crust from the fridge and carefully remove the top sheet of the parchment paper so that the crust is stuck to only the bottom sheet. Arrange your ramekins in a cluster together so that they all touch. Now, slip your hand under the parchment attached to the crust, and flip the parchment paper over the ramekins so that the pie crust is lying across all four ramekins. Using your hands, carefully press around the edge of each ramekin so that the pie crust sits directly on top of the filling. Remove the parchment paper and ensure that all the ramekins are covered. Using a paring knife, trim the crust to fit each of the ramekins. Discard the leftover dough (or you can save it and freeze it for anything else you may want pie crust for).

MAKE one small ½-inch slit in the center of each of the pie crusts. Using a pastry brush, carefully brush with the egg on the top of each crust. If desired, sprinkle with flaky salt.

SPREAD the ramekins apart on the baking sheet so that they are no longer touching and transfer to the oven. Bake until golden brown and crisp on top, 20 to 23 minutes.

LET cool for at least 10 minutes before serving. Garnish with thyme leaves, if desired.

Peruvian-Inspired Whole Roasted Chicken with Tangy Green Sauce

MAKES 4 SERVINGS • TOTAL TIME: 1 HOUR 15 MINUTES

This dish is inspired by one of the best rotisserie chicken spots in New York City: Pio Pio. They make an amazing Peruvian rotisserie chicken with ají verde sauce. Since I don't have a rotisserie, I roasted my chicken with a beautiful blend of spices, spatchcocked to cut down on the cooking time and to let the skin get super crispy. It's absolutely delicious by itself, but paired with this creamy and tangy green sauce, it's just outstanding!

FOR THE CHICKEN

1 whole chicken (3½ to 4 pounds)

2 teaspoons dried oregano

1½ teaspoons ground cumin

1 teaspoon paprika

½ teaspoon garlic powder

2 teaspoons kosher salt

1 teaspoon freshly ground black pepper

¼ cup avocado oil

FOR THE TANGY GREEN SAUCE

1 cup Homemade Mayo (page 251)

1 large jalapeño, seeded and roughly chopped

1 tablespoon distilled white vinegar

1 teaspoon kosher salt, plus more to taste

¼ teaspoon freshly ground black pepper, plus more to taste

2 garlic cloves, roughly chopped

½ cup loosely packed roughly chopped fresh cilantro

2 tablespoons freshly squeezed lime juice (about 1 lime)

COOK THE CHICKEN: Position a rack in the center of the oven and preheat the oven to 450°F.

PLACE the chicken on a cutting board, breast side down, so that the backbone is face up. Spatchcock the chicken (remove the backbone) by using a pair of good poultry shears to cut along both sides of the backbone. Start by cutting near the cavity of the chicken and continue in a straight line up toward the neck. Repeat on the other side of the backbone.

DISCARD the backbone (or save it for making stock). Flip the chicken over, breast side up, and use the heel of your hand to press down on the breastbone so that the chicken lies flat. Pat very dry with paper towels. Transfer the chicken skin side down to a large cast-iron skillet or sheet pan.

IN a small bowl, combine the oregano, cumin, paprika, garlic powder, salt, pepper, and avocado oil and stir until well combined.

BRUSH one-quarter of the seasoning mixture on the inside of the cavity. Flip the chicken over, skin side up, and pat dry one last time. Brush the remaining mixture evenly over the skin of the chicken.

TRANSFER the chicken to the oven and roast until cooked through or until a meat thermometer inserted into the thickest part of the breast registers 155° to 160°F, 35 to 45 minutes, depending on the size of the chicken. Let rest for at least 10 minutes before serving.

MEANWHILE, MAKE THE TANGY GREEN SAUCE: In a blender or using an immersion blender in a wide-mouth jar, combine the mayo, jalapeño, white vinegar, salt, pepper, garlic, cilantro, and lime juice. Blend until well combined.

FOR THE AVOCADO SALAD

2 tablespoons extra-virgin olive oil

1 teaspoon apple cider vinegar

2 tablespoons freshly squeezed lime juice (about 1 lime)

1 garlic clove, minced

Kosher salt and freshly ground black pepper, to taste

4 cups thinly sliced iceberg lettuce (about 1 large head)

1 large avocado, thinly sliced

1 large tomato on the vine, cut into thin wedges

½ English cucumber, thinly sliced on the diagonal

MAKE THE AVOCADO SALAD: In a small screw-top jar, combine the olive oil, apple cider vinegar, lime juice, garlic, and salt and pepper to taste. Shake to combine.

PLACE the lettuce in a large bowl or serving platter. Top with the sliced avocado, tomato, and cucumber. Drizzle with the dressing just before serving.

TO SERVE: Quarter the chicken and serve with the salad and tangy green sauce alongside.

FROM MY KITCHEN TO YOURS

TIME-SAVER: The green sauce can be made in advance and stored in the fridge for up to 1 week.

Paleo Lemon Chicken

MAKES 4 SERVINGS • TOTAL TIME: 45 MINUTES

This is such a fun takeout-inspired at-home dinner! The lemon sauce is thick and zingy, leaving a bright flavor in your mouth. This is very similar to orange chicken, which you may be more familiar with, but I highly recommend this lemon version, for an even sharper flavor. After you've tried the recipe as is, you can always sub in orange to change things up when you're craving takeout.

FOR THE LEMON SAUCE

¼ cup coconut aminos

¼ cup low-sodium chicken broth

1 tablespoon honey

Grated zest of ½ lemon

¼ cup freshly squeezed lemon juice (about 2 lemons)

½ teaspoon fish sauce

1 teaspoon toasted sesame oil

1-inch piece fresh ginger, peeled and finely grated

2 garlic cloves, minced

½ teaspoon crushed red pepper flakes

FOR THE CHICKEN

1½ pounds boneless, skinless chicken breast

1 teaspoon kosher salt

½ teaspoon ground white pepper

1 tablespoon coconut aminos

1 tablespoon plus ¼ cup avocado oil

1 egg white

⅓ cup tapioca flour

¼ cup sliced green onion, green parts only

2 tablespoons toasted sesame seeds

MAKE THE LEMON SAUCE: In a bowl, combine the coconut aminos, broth, honey, lemon zest, lemon juice, fish sauce, toasted sesame oil, ginger, garlic, and crushed red pepper flakes. Whisk until well combined. Set aside.

PREPARE THE CHICKEN: Place the chicken breasts on a cutting board and cover with parchment paper. Using a meat mallet or the bottom of a heavy skillet, pound the chicken to about a ¼-inch thickness. Pat the chicken dry with a paper towel. Cut the chicken into chunks about 1 inch square.

PLACE the chicken in a large bowl and add the salt, white pepper, coconut aminos, 1 tablespoon of the avocado oil, and the egg white. Stir until well combined. Set aside to marinate for 15 minutes.

PLACE the tapioca flour in a shallow bowl.

SHAKE the excess marinade off each chicken chunk, then dredge it in the tapioca flour to coat it evenly. Shake off any excess flour and set it on a sheet pan or large plate so that the following pieces will not touch. Repeat until all the chicken is coated.

IN a large nonstick skillet, heat the remaining ¼ cup avocado oil over medium-high heat. When the oil is hot but not yet smoking, carefully add the chicken pieces in a single layer, working in batches so as not to overcrowd the skillet. Cook until the chicken is a nice golden brown on each side and cooked through, about 3 minutes per side. Transfer the cooked pieces to a clean plate and repeat to brown the rest of the chicken.

REDUCE the heat under the skillet to medium and add the lemon sauce. Bring to a simmer, whisking constantly, and cook for about 2 minutes, until slightly thickened. Add the cooked chicken to the sauce and gently toss to combine. Cook, tossing gently, until the sauce has thickened and the chicken is very well coated with the sauce, 3 to 4 minutes.

REMOVE from the heat and toss in the green onions and toasted sesame seeds.

Panang Curry–Inspired Chicken Meatballs

GLUTEN-FREE
DAIRY-FREE
PALEO
WHOLE30
GRAIN-FREE

MAKES 4 SERVINGS • TOTAL TIME: 35 MINUTES

Traditionally, a Panang curry has a nutty, mellow flavor and texture from roasted peanuts ground directly into the curry paste. Here I've used almond butter—to keep it Whole30—combined with a delicious Thai red curry paste. When the meatballs absorb the sauce, it's a dreamy combination!

FOR THE MEATBALLS

- 2 pounds ground chicken thighs
- 2 tablespoons finely chopped fresh Thai basil
- 1 large egg, whisked
- 1 teaspoon kosher salt
- ½ teaspoon freshly ground black pepper
- ¼ cup almond flour
- 2 tablespoons avocado oil

FOR THE PANANG CURRY

- ¼ cup minced shallot (about 1 large shallot)
- 2 garlic cloves, minced
- 1-inch piece fresh ginger, peeled and finely grated
- 2 tablespoons Thai red curry paste (I like Mae Ploy brand)
- One 13.5-ounce can unsweetened full-fat coconut milk
- 1½ cups low-sodium chicken broth
- 3 tablespoons creamy almond butter (see note)
- 2 tablespoons coconut aminos
- 1 teaspoon fish sauce
- 2 tablespoons freshly squeezed lime juice (about 1 lime)
- ½ cup fresh Thai basil leaves, for serving
- 1 lime, cut into wedges, for serving

PAIRING SUGGESTION: Herby Rice Pilaf (page 200, sub prepared cauliflower rice for Whole30)

MAKE THE MEATBALLS: In a large bowl, combine the ground chicken, Thai basil, egg, salt, pepper, and almond flour. Mix until just combined. Using damp hands, form the mixture into 2-inch meatballs. (Damp hands keep the meat from sticking too much.)

IN a large deep skillet, heat the oil over medium-high heat until shimmering. Add the meatballs, working in batches as needed so as not to overcrowd the pan, and cook on each side until golden brown, 2 to 3 minutes per side. The meatballs don't have to be fully cooked through, as they will continue to cook in the sauce. Transfer the browned meatballs to a plate and set aside.

MAKE THE PANANG CURRY: Reduce the heat under the skillet to medium. Add the shallot, garlic, and ginger and cook, stirring often, until the shallot is tender, 2 to 3 minutes. Add the red curry paste and continue to cook until the paste is softened and fragrant, about 2 minutes. While whisking, slowly pour in the coconut milk and continue to whisk until the mixture is clump-free. Add the broth, almond butter, coconut aminos, and fish sauce. Bring the sauce to a simmer and continue whisking until the sauce is very smooth, 1 to 2 minutes. Nestle the meatballs into the sauce and simmer, covered, until the meatballs are cooked through and the flavors have melded, about 10 minutes.

STIR in the lime juice and Thai basil. Serve over Herby Rice Pilaf, if desired, and with a wedge of lime.

FROM MY KITCHEN TO YOURS

If you prefer to use peanut butter instead of almond butter, use only 2 tablespoons! Just keep in mind that peanut butter is not considered Whole30 or paleo compatible.

Creamy Chicken Toscana

MAKES 4 SERVINGS • TOTAL TIME: 45 MINUTES

This is one of my go-to weeknight dinners. It's healthy, it's comforting, my whole family loves it, and it's all made in one skillet! Borrowing the flavors of a creamy Zuppa Toscana (page 70), this chicken dish is a creamy and dreamy twist on the Italian classic you're sure to love for a quick, hearty meal.

3 slices thick-cut bacon, minced

2 pounds boneless, skinless chicken breasts

1½ teaspoons kosher salt

½ teaspoon freshly ground black pepper

¼ cup cassava flour

1 tablespoon ghee (sub vegan butter for dairy-free)

½ cup halved and thinly sliced shallot (about 1 large shallot)

3 garlic cloves, minced

¼ teaspoon crushed red pepper flakes

2½ cups (20 ounces) low-sodium chicken broth

2 tablespoons freshly squeezed lemon juice (about 1 lemon)

2 teaspoons Dijon mustard

1 teaspoon Italian seasoning

2 cups peeled and diced (¼-inch) russet potato (about 1 large potato)

2 cups deribbed and thinly sliced lacinato kale (about ½ large bunch)

¾ cup unsweetened full-fat coconut milk or dairy-free creamer

1 lemon, cut into wedges, for serving

IN a large deep nonstick skillet, cook the bacon over medium heat until just crisp, 3 to 4 minutes. Using a slotted spoon, transfer the cooked bacon to a plate lined with paper towels and set aside, reserving the fat in the bottom of the skillet.

MEANWHILE, place the chicken breasts on a cutting board and cover with parchment paper. Using a meat mallet or the bottom of a heavy skillet, pound the chicken breasts to a ¼-inch thickness. Pat dry with a paper towel. Season the chicken with 1 teaspoon of the salt and the black pepper.

SET the skillet with the bacon fat over medium-high heat. Place the cassava flour in a bowl and dredge each chicken breast so that it is evenly coated, shaking off any excess. Carefully place the chicken in the skillet and cook until golden brown and cooked through, about 4 minutes per side. You may need to work in two batches to avoid crowding the pan. Transfer the cooked chicken to a plate and set aside.

REDUCE the heat under the pan to medium. Add the ghee and let it melt. Add the shallot, garlic, and pepper flakes and cook until the shallot is tender, about 2 minutes, stirring often and taking care that it doesn't burn.

ADD the chicken broth, lemon juice, mustard, Italian seasoning, and remaining ½ teaspoon salt and stir until well combined, scraping up any browned bits from the bottom of the pan. Bring the sauce to a simmer. Add the potato, cover, and cook until tender, 15 to 18 minutes.

ADD the kale and coconut milk and stir until the kale is slightly wilted, about 2 minutes. Add the cooked bacon and nestle the chicken into the sauce. Cover and cook until the chicken is heated through, about 5 minutes. Serve with lemon wedges on the side.

Chicken Quesadillas with
Creamy Jalapeño Sauce

MAKES 4 SERVINGS • TOTAL TIME: 35 MINUTES

If you've had the chicken quesadilla from Taco Bell, you know how delicious it is. It's rather simple: a flour tortilla grilled with a combination of cheese, chicken, and just one special touch—the secret is the sauce! Oh my goodness, that creamy jalapeño sauce just puts a classic chicken and cheese quesadilla over the top! I've re-created that special sauce and quesadilla in my own kitchen and it's just as delicious. The perfect meal for a busy weeknight, late-night meal, or hungover morning!

FOR THE CREAMY JALAPEÑO SAUCE

½ cup Homemade Mayo (page 251)

2 garlic cloves, peeled

2 tablespoons hot sauce (I use Tapatío)

½ cup drained sliced mild pickled jalapeños (from a jar)

1 tablespoon freshly squeezed lime juice (about ½ lime)

1 teaspoon distilled white vinegar

1 teaspoon onion powder

½ teaspoon garlic powder

¼ teaspoon smoked paprika

¼ teaspoon kosher salt

FOR THE CHICKEN FILLING

2 tablespoons avocado oil

1 pound boneless, skinless chicken breast, cut into ½-inch chunks

1 teaspoon kosher salt

½ teaspoon freshly ground black pepper

½ teaspoon ground cumin

1 teaspoon chili powder

FOR THE QUESADILLAS

2 tablespoons avocado oil

4 grain-free burrito-size tortillas (I use Siete brand)

1⅓ cups freshly shredded sharp cheddar cheese

1⅓ cups freshly shredded Monterey Jack cheese

MAKE THE CREAMY JALAPEÑO SAUCE: In a food processor or blender, combine the mayo, garlic, hot sauce, jalapeños, lime juice, vinegar, onion powder, garlic powder, smoked paprika, and salt and blend until completely smooth. Set aside. (This keeps for 5 to 7 days in the refrigerator.)

MAKE THE CHICKEN FILLING: In a large skillet, heat the avocado oil over medium-high heat. When the skillet is hot, add the diced chicken, salt, pepper, cumin, and chili powder. Toss to combine. Cook, tossing occasionally, until the chicken is golden brown on all sides, 5 to 7 minutes. Transfer to a plate and set aside.

MAKE THE QUESADILLAS: You'll be making one quesadilla at a time. In a large nonstick skillet, heat ½ tablespoon of the avocado oil over medium heat, lay the tortilla in the oil, and quickly fry on each side until flexible and easy to fold, about 30 seconds on each side.

CAREFULLY spread about ¼ cup of the jalapeño sauce over it, ensuring that the sauce reaches the edges. To one half of the tortilla, add ⅓ cup of the chicken, ⅓ cup of the cheddar, and ⅓ cup of the Monterey Jack. Gently fold the tortilla in half to form a quesadilla.

COOK until golden brown on one side, 2 to 3 minutes. Using a large spatula, carefully flip the quesadilla and cook on the other side until golden brown, 2 to 3 more minutes.

TRANSFER to a plate lined with paper towels. Repeat to assemble and cook the remaining three quesadillas, adding ½ tablespoon of oil to the pan with each batch. When all of the quesadillas are cooked, cut into thirds and serve with any remaining sauce for dipping.

Thai-Inspired Chicken Fried Rice

MAKES 2 SERVINGS • TOTAL TIME: 30 MINUTES

When you have leftover rice, there is nothing better than whipping up a batch of fried rice. I really love this Thai-inspired version. It's got a little spice from the Thai chiles, lots of salty-umami flavors from the fish sauce and coconut aminos, a little zing from the lime, and tons of fresh herbs. This is definitely a staple in our home when we have leftover rice and rotisserie chicken. It all comes together in 30 minutes!

2 tablespoons avocado oil

3 garlic cloves, minced

½ cup halved and thinly sliced shallot (about 1 large shallot)

½ cup minced carrot (about 1 carrot)

1 to 3 thinly sliced fresh Thai chiles (1 for mild, 3 for hot)

1 cup diced cooked chicken (store-bought rotisserie or Fauxtisserie Chicken, page 247)

4 green onions, cut on the diagonal into 2-inch lengths (about 1 cup)

1 teaspoon kosher salt

½ teaspoon ground white pepper

2 cups chilled cooked rice (see note)

2 teaspoons toasted sesame seeds

2 tablespoons coconut aminos

2 tablespoons fish sauce

2 eggs, well whisked

2 tablespoons freshly squeezed lime juice (about 1 lime)

¼ cup loosely packed chopped fresh cilantro leaves, plus more for serving

¼ cup loosely packed chopped fresh mint leaves

¼ cup loosely packed chopped fresh Thai basil leaves

½ cup thinly sliced cucumber, for serving

1 lime, cut into wedges, for serving

IN a large nonstick skillet, heat the avocado oil over medium-high heat. Add the garlic, shallot, carrot, and Thai chiles and cook, stirring, until the veggies are just tender, about 3 minutes. Add the diced chicken, green onions, salt, white pepper, rice, and sesame seeds and stir to combine. Spread the rice into a single layer, press down with your spatula, and cook undisturbed until golden brown on the bottom, 2 to 3 minutes.

ADD the coconut aminos and fish sauce and cook, stirring to combine and let the sauce soak into the rice, about 2 minutes.

PUSH the rice to one half of the skillet and pour the eggs onto the empty half. Cook the eggs, stirring, until softly scrambled, 1 to 2 minutes. Stir the scrambled eggs into the rice until well combined.

REMOVE the skillet from the heat and stir in the lime juice, cilantro, mint, and Thai basil.

SERVE topped with cucumber slices, cilantro leaves, and a wedge of lime.

FROM MY KITCHEN TO YOURS

When cooking any sort of fried rice, leftover, day-old rice works best. When rice is freshly cooked, it retains a lot of moisture, which makes it difficult to crisp up. If you're making the rice the same day, make a batch of rice and spread it in a thin layer on a sheet pan. Put the tray in the refrigerator and let it sit for 30 to 60 minutes to dry out the rice as much as possible before frying.

Crunchy Chicken Tinga Tacos

MAKES 4 SERVINGS • TOTAL TIME: 45 MINUTES

If you've been cooking from my blog for a while, you know I love making crunchy tacos like this: taking tortillas, stuffing them with a delicious filling, and throwing them into the oven. You end up with a soft center that holds together surrounded by crispy edges. So good! Here, I've stuffed them with the most delicious, quick-and-easy chicken tinga filling. It's tangy, spicy, and just delicious. This is a showstopping taco recipe for sure!

FOR THE FILLING

One 14.5-ounce can diced fire-roasted tomatoes

3 garlic cloves, peeled

2½ teaspoons chipotle chile powder

1 teaspoon smoked paprika

½ teaspoon ground cumin

2 tablespoons apple cider vinegar

2 teaspoons coconut sugar

1 teaspoon kosher salt

½ cup halved and thinly sliced white onion (about ½ small onion)

4 cups finely shredded rotisserie chicken (store-bought or Fauxtisserie Chicken, page 247)

1 tablespoon freshly squeezed lime juice (about ½ lime)

FOR THE TACOS

½ teaspoon avocado oil, plus more as needed

8 grain-free tortillas (I use Siete brand)

1 cup shredded romaine lettuce

¼ cup minced white onion (about ¼ small onion)

½ cup crumbled queso fresco or Cotija cheese (omit for dairy-free)

2 tablespoons chopped fresh cilantro

1 lime, cut into wedges, for serving

PAIRING SUGGESTIONS: **Shrimp Ceviche (page 20), Clayton's Margarita (page 230)**

PREHEAT the oven to 400°F. Line a sheet pan with parchment paper.

MAKE THE FILLING: In a food processor or blender, combine the tomatoes, garlic, chipotle powder, smoked paprika, cumin, vinegar, and coconut sugar. Blend until completely smooth.

POUR the tomato mixture into a medium saucepan over medium heat and add the salt and onion. Bring to a simmer and cook, stirring often, until the onion is tender, about 10 minutes.

REDUCE the heat to low under the saucepan. Add the chicken and lime juice and stir until the chicken is well coated. Simmer, uncovered and stirring occasionally, until the chicken is very tender and has absorbed the flavor from the sauce, about 4 minutes. Set aside to cool before filling the tacos.

ASSEMBLE THE TACOS: In a small nonstick skillet, heat the avocado oil over medium-high heat. Quickly fry each tortilla, about 30 seconds on each side, until flexible and easy to fold.

SET a tortilla on the lined sheet pan and scoop about ½ cup of the chicken mixture onto one side of the tortilla. Gently fold the tortilla in half and press down, forming a taco. Continue frying, filling, and folding the tacos, adding more oil to the skillet as needed, until you've used all the filling.

BAKE until the tacos are crispy and golden brown on the edges, 10 to 12 minutes.

REMOVE the tacos from the oven. Very gently open the tacos and fill with the shredded lettuce, white onion, queso fresco (if using), and cilantro. Serve with lime wedges.

seafood

Tuna Tostadas with Chipotle Aioli and Crispy Leeks

MAKES 4 SERVINGS • TOTAL TIME: 30 MINUTES

Imagine yourself dining al fresco on a warm summer day with an ice-cold beer and these deliciously fresh tuna tostadas. What a treat! These tostadas are a household favorite here. The inspiration for them came from a fantastic restaurant in Mexico City, Contramar. The ingredients are simple yet they come together brightly and beautifully!

1 pound sushi-grade tuna, very thinly sliced against the grain

4 tablespoons avocado oil

2 tablespoons coconut aminos

½ cup Homemade Mayo (page 251)

2 garlic cloves, peeled

2 teaspoons chipotle chile powder

2 tablespoons freshly squeezed lime juice (about 1 lime)

Pinch of kosher salt

Pinch of freshly ground black pepper

1 small leek, white and light-green parts only, thinly sliced

8 grain-free tortillas (I use Siete brand)

Avocado oil spray

2 tablespoons cassava flour

1 avocado, cut into very thin strips

Flaky salt

1 lime, cut into wedges, for serving

Cilantro leaves, for garnish

PREHEAT the oven to 375°F. Line two sheet pans with parchment paper.

IN a large shallow bowl, combine the tuna, 2 tablespoons of the avocado oil, and the coconut aminos. Set aside to let the fish marinate while you make the aioli.

IN a food processor or blender, combine the mayo, garlic, chipotle powder, lime juice, salt, and black pepper. Blend until smooth and set the aioli aside.

PLACE the sliced leeks in a colander and run hot water over them until they are well rinsed. Place the leeks on paper towels and pat dry. Set aside.

PLACE the tortillas on the prepared sheet pans and mist the tops with avocado oil spray. Bake until the tortillas are crisp and golden brown on the edges, about 8 minutes.

MEANWHILE, in a large nonstick skillet, heat the remaining 2 tablespoons avocado oil over medium-high heat. Place the leeks in a bowl and sprinkle with the cassava flour. Toss until the leeks are evenly coated. When the oil is hot, add half the leeks to the skillet in a single layer and fry until golden brown and crisp, tossing halfway through, 3 to 4 minutes total. Transfer the crispy leeks to a plate lined with paper towels. Repeat for a second batch of leeks. You will likely need to clean the skillet and use fresh oil for the second batch to prevent burning.

TO ASSEMBLE: Spread a thin layer of aioli on each crisp tortilla. Next, in this order, top with 3 to 4 slices of the tuna, a few slices of avocado, some crispy leeks, and a sprinkle of flaky salt. Serve with lime wedges and garnish with cilantro.

Herby Green Curry Poached Halibut

GLUTEN-FREE
DAIRY-FREE
PALEO
WHOLE30 (IF MODIFIED)
GRAIN-FREE (IF MODIFIED)

MAKES 4 SERVINGS • TOTAL TIME: 20 MINUTES

Green curry paste is one of my favorite pantry staples. This popular Thai curry paste not only has a spicy kick to it but is also packed with vibrant herbs and aromatics like garlic and ginger, making it a great way to get a delightful dinner loaded with flavor on the table with very little effort. A good curry paste does just about all the work! Here, the fish is cooked in the coconut green curry broth to infuse it with the aromatics while also leaving the fish melt-in-your-mouth tender. The fish, broth, and fresh herbs ladled over jasmine rice are a real delight that I love any night of the week, but especially when it's cold outside.

2 tablespoons avocado oil

2 small shallots, thinly sliced

2 garlic cloves, thinly sliced

2 tablespoons Thai green curry paste (I like Mae Ploy brand)

1 cup unsweetened full-fat coconut milk

¾ cup low-sodium seafood stock

2 teaspoons fish sauce

Grated zest of 1 lime

1½ pounds skinless halibut, cod, or other white flaky fish fillet, cut into 4-inch pieces

1 tablespoon freshly squeezed lime juice (about ½ lime)

½ cup roughly chopped fresh cilantro leaves and tender stems

¼ cup fresh mint leaves

¼ cup fresh Thai basil leaves

2 cups steamed jasmine rice, for serving (sub cauliflower rice for Whole30, paleo, and grain-free)

1 lime, cut into wedges, for serving

PAIRING SUGGESTION: **Sesame Asparagus Sauté (page 196)**

IN a large deep skillet, heat the oil over medium heat. Add the shallots and garlic and sauté until the shallots are tender, about 3 minutes. Add the green curry paste. Using the back of a spoon, break up the curry paste, toasting it in the oil until very fragrant, about 2 minutes.

ADD the coconut milk, seafood stock, fish sauce, and lime zest. Whisk until well combined and bring the mixture to a simmer. Carefully place the halibut pieces into the curry broth. Cover and cook until the fish is cooked through and flaky, 4 to 5 minutes. Add the lime juice, cilantro, mint, and Thai basil.

TO SERVE: Ladle the fish and broth in a bowl over steamed rice. Serve with lime wedges.

FROM MY KITCHEN TO YOURS

Have leftover green curry paste? Try making the Creamy Cauliflower Green Curry Soup (page 54).

Salmon al Pastor

MAKES 4 SERVINGS • TOTAL TIME: 40 MINUTES

While I don't like to pick favorites, this is one of my very favorite recipes in this book. This dish borrows the flavors of al pastor, a popular Mexican style of taco containing marinated pork or lamb cooked on vertical spits. The warming spice blend combined with the sweet and tart pineapple is fantastic on just about any protein—but this easy salmon weeknight dinner is delightful in every way. It's light, easy, and very flavorful!

2 garlic cloves, peeled

¾ cup small-diced fresh pineapple

1 teaspoon distilled white vinegar

2 teaspoons ancho chile powder or chipotle chile powder

1 teaspoon chili powder

¼ teaspoon ground cumin

¼ teaspoon dried oregano

¼ teaspoon ground cinnamon

2 tablespoons freshly squeezed lime juice (about 1 lime)

2 tablespoons freshly squeezed orange juice (about ½ orange)

¼ cup low-sodium chicken broth

¾ teaspoon kosher salt

2 tablespoons avocado oil

4 center-cut salmon fillets (6 to 8 ounces each)

¼ teaspoon freshly ground black pepper

Quick-Pickled Red Onions (page 248)

¼ cup roughly chopped fresh cilantro leaves, optional for serving

1 tablespoon thinly sliced serrano pepper, optional for serving

PAIRING SUGGESTIONS: Herby Rice Pilaf (page 200), Mezcal Mule (page 234)

IN a food processor or blender, combine the garlic, ¼ cup of the diced pineapple, the vinegar, ancho powder, chili powder, cumin, oregano, cinnamon, lime juice, orange juice, broth, and ¼ teaspoon of the salt. Blend the pastor sauce until smooth.

IN a nonstick skillet, heat the avocado oil over medium-high heat. Season the salmon with the remaining ½ teaspoon salt and the pepper. Place the salmon in the hot skillet and cook until golden brown on each side, about 2 minutes per side. Reduce the heat to medium and pour the pastor sauce around the salmon in the skillet, along with the remaining ½ cup diced pineapple.

CONTINUE to cook the salmon, uncovered and simmering, until just cooked through, 3 to 4 minutes.

TRANSFER the salmon to a large serving platter and pour the sauce over the fillets. Top with the pickled red onions. If desired, garnish with cilantro and a few slices of serrano pepper if you're feeling extra spicy!

Shrimp Brochette Skillet with Poblano Rice

GLUTEN-FREE
DAIRY-FREE (IF MODIFIED)

MAKES 4 SERVINGS • TOTAL TIME: 25 MINUTES

FOR THE POBLANO RICE

2 tablespoons avocado oil

1 cup medium-diced white onion (about ½ medium onion)

1 cup medium-diced seeded poblano pepper (1 large poblano)

3 garlic cloves, minced

1 teaspoon kosher salt

½ teaspoon freshly ground black pepper

2 cups (16 ounces) low-sodium vegetable broth

1 cup loosely packed fresh cilantro leaves

2 cups white jasmine or other long-grain white rice

FOR THE SHRIMP BROCHETTE

5 slices bacon, cut into 1-inch pieces

1½ pounds shrimp (31/40 count), peeled and deveined, patted dry

2 garlic cloves, thinly sliced

½ large jalapeño, thinly sliced

½ teaspoon kosher salt

¼ teaspoon freshly ground black pepper

1 tablespoon unsalted butter or ghee (sub vegan butter for dairy-free)

1 tablespoon roughly chopped fresh oregano leaves

1 lime, cut into wedges

Have you ever had shrimp brochette? It's essentially shrimp stuffed with jalapeño, wrapped in bacon, and grilled. Fantastic! Well, this shrimp dish is a deconstructed skillet rendition and oh my, it is good! My version takes less prep time than the traditional method and gives you crispy bacon without having to worry about overcooking the shrimp. But what really sets it over the top is the poblano rice! Once you've tried this poblano rice, you're going to want it with everything. It's so easy to make and I love its unique, vibrant flavor! The two together make for a total showstopper.

MAKE THE POBLANO RICE: In a large saucepan, heat the avocado oil over medium heat. Add the onion, poblano, garlic, salt, and black pepper and cook, stirring often, until the vegetables are tender, about 5 minutes. Transfer the sautéed veggies to a food processor or blender. Add 1 cup of the vegetable broth and the cilantro and blend until smooth.

POUR the poblano mixture into the same saucepan you cooked the veggies in and add the remaining 1 cup vegetable broth and the rice. Stir to combine and bring to a boil over medium-high heat. Reduce the heat to a low simmer, cover, and cook for 15 minutes. Remove from the heat and let rest, covered, for 10 minutes while you prepare the shrimp.

MEANWHILE, MAKE THE SHRIMP BROCHETTE: Heat a large skillet over medium-high heat. Add the bacon and cook, tossing occasionally, until it just crisps, about 5 minutes. Drain off any excess bacon fat, reserving about 2 tablespoons in the skillet.

ADD the shrimp, garlic, jalapeño, salt, and black pepper to the skillet with the bacon and bacon fat. Cook the shrimp over medium-high heat until they are just cooked through and golden brown, 2 to 3 minutes per side. You may need to work in two batches to avoid crowding the pan. Add all the shrimp back into the skillet along with the butter, let the butter melt, and toss to combine. Sprinkle with the oregano.

TO SERVE: Fluff the poblano rice with a fork and divide among 4 plates. Spoon the shrimp and its juices over the poblano rice. Serve with a lime wedge.

Paleo Battered Fish Tacos

MAKES 4 SERVINGS • TOTAL TIME: 30 MINUTES

FOR THE BATTER

½ cup plus 1 tablespoon cassava flour

2 tablespoons tapioca or arrowroot flour

1½ teaspoons kosher salt

½ teaspoon smoked paprika

1 teaspoon onion powder

1 cup cold Topo Chico (or any unflavored sparkling water)

FOR THE SLAW

¼ cup Homemade Mayo (page 251)

2 tablespoons freshly squeezed lime juice (about 1 lime)

2 garlic cloves, minced

2 teaspoons your favorite hot sauce (I use El Yucateco)

½ teaspoon kosher salt

3 cups shredded cabbage or slaw mix

½ cup chopped fresh cilantro, plus more for garnish

FOR THE FISH

⅓ cup avocado oil

1½ pounds skinless halibut or cod fillet, cut into 2- to 3-inch pieces

Kosher salt, to taste

FOR THE TACOS

12 grain-free tortillas (I use Siete brand)

Pico de gallo or salsa

1 lime, cut into wedges

Quick-Pickled Red Onions (page 248), optional for serving

If you have anyone in your life who is on the fence about seafood, here's a recipe to help sway them. Just like beer, the bubbles from the Topo Chico add body and lightness to the batter, but keep things paleo. You can use another unflavored sparkling water, but Topo Chico is the most effervescent—and my very favorite. I also use a mix of cassava flour and arrowroot flour for the breading to keep the recipe grain-free and gluten-free, along with a few seasonings to add flavor. Beware— the result might just make your taco-loving heart explode!

MAKE THE BATTER: In a large bowl, combine the cassava flour, tapioca flour, salt, smoked paprika, and onion powder and whisk so that there are no longer any clumps. Pour in the sparkling water and whisk until well combined. Set aside to thicken up for at least 5 minutes while you prepare the slaw. When it's ready, the batter should have the consistency of a pancake batter. It should flow smoothly from the whisk, a little heavier than chocolate milk but thinner than cake batter. (Please see my note on best batter tips.)

MAKE THE SLAW: To make the slaw dressing, in a large bowl, whisk together the mayo, lime juice, garlic, hot sauce, and salt until well combined. Toss the cabbage and cilantro in the slaw dressing until well coated. Set aside until you're ready to serve.

COOK THE FISH: In a large nonstick skillet, heat the avocado oil over medium to medium-high heat. Pat the fish very dry with a paper towel. Place half the fish pieces in the batter and gently toss to coat.

WHEN the oil is hot and shimmering but not smoking, use a fork or tongs to pick up one piece of battered fish at a time, shaking off any excess batter, and carefully place the fish in the hot oil. You'll want to work in batches so as not to overcrowd the skillet. If your pan is on the smaller side, do three batches instead of two. Let the fish fry until golden brown on both sides and cooked through, 2 to 3 minutes per side.

TRANSFER the cooked fish to a large plate lined with paper towels and sprinkle with a pinch of salt to finish. Repeat until all the fish is browned. If your oil starts to smoke from excess batter, pour out the oil between batches, wipe out the pan with a paper towel, and use an additional ⅓ cup of oil.

FROM MY KITCHEN TO YOURS

BATTER TIPS: Cassava flour can be a little fickle, so here are a few notes. The temperature of the sparkling water makes a difference. If you use cold water right out of the fridge, your recipe will likely turn out perfect. If you use room temperature, your batter might be thinner. The brand of cassava flour may change the recipe a tad, too. If your batter is too thin, add 2 to 4 more tablespoons of cassava. If it's too thick, add ¼ cup more sparkling water! Keep in mind the batter will thicken as it sits. Before battering the second batch of fish, you may need to add a splash of sparkling water to counteract this!

FRYING TIPS: It's very important to use a good nonstick pan here. In a heavy-bottomed or cast-iron pan, your fish will likely stick to the bottom and fall apart. You don't need a thermometer for shallow-frying; to see if your oil is hot enough, drop a teeny bit of batter into the oil as a test. If it begins to fry immediately, you're good to go. If you fry the fish before the oil is hot, your batter will be soaked with oil and won't crisp up.

TO SERVE: One at a time, place the tortillas in a dry (no oil) stainless steel skillet over medium heat and cook for about 30 seconds on each side. You can also do away with the skillet and char the tortillas directly over a gas flame for a few seconds using tongs.

FOR each taco, place a small amount of the slaw in the bottom of a warm tortilla and top with a piece of fish. Garnish with pico de gallo, cilantro, a squeeze of lime, and pickled onions (if using). You can always serve with more hot sauce, too, if you want.

Israeli Couscous with Clams

MAKES 4 SERVINGS • TOTAL TIME: 25 MINUTES

While you can never go wrong with linguine and clams, Israeli couscous with clams is a great idea, too. I love that this dish straddles the line between a little stew and a little pasta situation. The flavors are simple, elegant, and delightful. I will say, if you're in a bind and doing a little pantry diving in order to make dinner happen, canned clams alone will still taste fantastic. But, of course, the fresh clams are a beautiful touch in this dish! And heads up—if you're using fresh clams, be sure to wash them well, as noted below.

2 tablespoons extra-virgin olive oil

1½ cups halved and thinly sliced white onion (about 1 medium onion)

4 garlic cloves, thinly sliced

1 teaspoon kosher salt

½ teaspoon freshly ground black pepper

½ teaspoon crushed red pepper flakes

8 oil-packed anchovy fillets (or 4 teaspoons anchovy paste)

2 tablespoons tomato paste

1 cup dry white wine

4 cups (32 ounces) seafood stock

20 saffron threads

1½ cups Israeli couscous

One 10-ounce can whole baby clams, drained

2 pounds littleneck clams, rinsed very well (see note)

¼ cup finely chopped fresh parsley leaves, plus more for garnish

Grated zest and juice of 1 lemon

1 lemon, cut into wedges, for serving

IN a large deep skillet, heat the oil over medium heat. When the oil is shimmering, add the onion, garlic, salt, black pepper, and pepper flakes. Cook, stirring, until the onion is tender and golden, 5 to 7 minutes.

ADD the anchovy fillets and continue to cook, stirring and mashing up the fillets, until they break down into a paste, about 2 minutes. Add the tomato paste and stir until well combined, then cook for about 1 minute to cook out the raw tomato taste, stirring often.

ADD the wine, stock, and saffron and bring to a boil. Add the couscous and reduce the heat to a rapid simmer. Cook, uncovered and stirring occasionally, until the couscous is par-cooked and slightly tender, about 6 minutes.

REDUCE the heat to a gentle simmer and add the canned clams, fresh clams, and parsley. Cook, covered, until the fresh clams open, 4 to 6 minutes. Discard any unopened clams. Add the lemon zest and juice and stir to combine.

LADLE into bowls and serve with lemon wedges on the side. Garnish with parsley.

FROM MY KITCHEN TO YOURS

Never cooked with fresh clams before? When you bring them home from the fishmonger, they will still be alive. Remove them from the bag immediately, put them in an open container, and place them in the fridge, uncovered, until you're ready to use them (they will last 1 to 2 days when stored properly). It's also essential that you clean them very well or your dish could have little bits of sand in it, which kind of defeats the purpose of this guest-worthy dish. To clean, place the clams in a bowl and cover them with cool tap water. Let the clams sit for 20 minutes to 1 hour. During this time, the clams will expel sand from inside their shells. When you're ready to cook, lift each clam from the water and rinse it, scrubbing if necessary, to get rid of any grit on the outside of the shell.

Clayton's Favorite Mustard Salmon

MAKES 4 SERVINGS • TOTAL TIME: 30 MINUTES

FOR THE MUSTARD SAUCE

2 tablespoons grainy mustard

1 tablespoon Dijon mustard

1 tablespoon brine from a jar of pepperoncini (sub 1 teaspoon apple cider vinegar for Whole30)

1 teaspoon fresh thyme leaves

FOR THE CAULIFLOWER PUREE

4 cups cauliflower florets (about 1 large head)

2 garlic cloves, peeled

1 cup low-sodium chicken broth

1 teaspoon fresh thyme leaves

1 teaspoon kosher salt

½ teaspoon freshly ground black pepper

¼ cup unsweetened full-fat coconut milk

FOR THE SALMON

2 tablespoons extra-virgin olive oil

4 center-cut salmon fillets (6 ounces each), skin removed

1½ teaspoons kosher salt

½ teaspoon freshly ground black pepper

FOR THE CRISPY SHALLOTS

1 tablespoon extra-virgin olive oil, optional

2 large shallots, thinly sliced

2 tablespoons cassava flour

½ teaspoon kosher salt

PAIRING SUGGESTION: Parmesan-Roasted Zucchini (page 195)

Here's a salmon dish that's very easy to prepare but will make you feel like you're dining at a great restaurant. All the flavors are simple, yet they come together just beautifully. After I created this dish, my husband began requesting it weekly, making it "Clayton's Favorite"!

MAKE THE MUSTARD SAUCE: In a small bowl, stir together the grainy mustard, Dijon, pepperoncini brine, and thyme leaves. Refrigerate until ready to serve. (This keeps well for up to 2 weeks in the refrigerator.)

MAKE THE CAULIFLOWER PUREE: In a medium saucepan, combine the cauliflower, garlic, broth, thyme, salt, and pepper. Bring to a boil over medium-high heat. Reduce the heat to a simmer, cover, and cook until the cauliflower is fork-tender, 12 to 14 minutes.

CAREFULLY transfer the cauliflower, along with the contents of the saucepan, to a blender or food processor. Add the coconut milk and blend until smooth, about 30 seconds. Cover to keep warm.

COOK THE SALMON: In a large nonstick skillet, heat the oil over medium-high heat. Pat the salmon fillets dry and season all sides with the salt and pepper. When the skillet is hot but not smoking, place the salmon on one side, searing until the salmon is golden brown, about 3 minutes. Flip the salmon and cook to your desired doneness, about 3 minutes for medium or about 4 minutes for well-done, depending on the thickness of your fillets. Transfer the cooked salmon to a plate and set aside.

MAKE THE CRISPY SHALLOTS: Reduce the heat under the skillet to medium-low. If needed, add the 1 tablespoon of oil. In a small bowl, combine the sliced shallots, cassava flour, and salt and toss until well coated. Working in batches as needed, spread the shallots into a single layer in the skillet and fry until crisp, 2 to 3 minutes, flipping halfway through. Transfer to a plate lined with paper towels to absorb the extra oil.

TO SERVE: Smear the cauliflower puree onto individual plates, spreading it into a thin layer. Place the salmon on top. Spoon the mustard sauce over the salmon and top with the crispy shallots.

Shrimp Étouffée

MAKES 4 SERVINGS • TOTAL TIME: 25 MINUTES

2 tablespoons avocado oil

1½ pounds shrimp (31/40 count), peeled, deveined, and tails off

1 teaspoon kosher salt

½ teaspoon freshly ground black pepper

2 tablespoons ghee (sub vegan butter for dairy-free)

2 tablespoons arrowroot flour

1 cup minced yellow onion (about ½ medium onion)

¾ cup minced celery (about 1 large stalk)

¾ cup minced green bell pepper (about ½ medium bell pepper)

4 green onions, thinly sliced

1 teaspoon dried oregano

1 teaspoon dried rosemary

1 teaspoon dried thyme

1 teaspoon paprika

½ teaspoon cayenne pepper

¼ teaspoon crushed red pepper flakes

One 14.5-ounce can diced tomatoes, drained

1 teaspoon fish sauce

2 cups (16 ounces) low-sodium chicken broth or seafood stock

1 bay leaf

Cooked packaged cauliflower rice (sub steamed white rice if not Whole30 or grain-free), for serving

¼ cup chopped fresh parsley, for serving

Louisiana-style hot sauce, for serving (I like Crystal)

This shrimp étouffée recipe has been on the blog for quite some time, and it's definitely one of the Defined Dish community's favorites. I just love the big, bold flavors of Louisiana cooking, and this dish has it going on! It's healthy, simple to make, and incredibly flavorful. This dish comes together quickly, so it's helpful to have the veggies chopped and spices measured out before you get started.

IN a large nonstick skillet, heat the oil over medium-high heat. Pat the shrimp dry with a paper towel. When the oil is shimmering and hot, add the shrimp in a single layer and season with the salt and pepper. Cook the shrimp until just cooked through, about 2 minutes per side. Transfer the cooked shrimp to a plate and set aside.

REDUCE the heat under the skillet to medium and add the ghee to melt. Add the arrowroot flour and stir, pressing all the clumps out with the edge of a spoon, until the mixture is smooth. Add the onion, celery, bell pepper, and three-quarters of the green onions and season with the oregano, rosemary, thyme, paprika, cayenne, and pepper flakes. Cook, stirring, until the vegetables are tender and the spices are fragrant, about 4 minutes.

ADD the diced tomatoes, fish sauce, and broth and stir until just incorporated. Add the bay leaf and bring to a rapid simmer.

COOK, uncovered and stirring often, scraping up the browned bits from the bottom of the pan, for 5 to 7 minutes to reduce and thicken the sauce a bit.

REDUCE the heat to low and return the shrimp to the skillet. Stir to combine. Taste and adjust seasoning, if desired. Discard the bay leaf.

SERVE over prepared cauliflower rice and garnish with parsley, the remaining green onions, and hot sauce to taste.

Miso-Broiled Halibut

GLUTEN-FREE
DAIRY-FREE

MAKES 4 SERVINGS • TOTAL TIME: 20 MINUTES

Miso paste is one of my favorite ways to add umami to any weeknight dinner. This miso-broiled halibut could not be easier to make and is so delicious. It comes together in just 20 minutes and is great served alongside jasmine or cauliflower rice to help soak up the sauce! I know fish can be intimidating for home cooks, but this simple broiler method keeps it fast and easy.

FOR THE WHITE WINE MISO SAUCE

¼ cup white wine

2 tablespoons coconut sugar or cane sugar

¼ cup gluten-free white miso (see note on page 43)

½ cup coconut aminos

¼ cup low-sodium chicken broth or seafood stock

1 tablespoon freshly squeezed lime juice (about ½ lime)

1-inch piece fresh ginger, grated

FOR THE HALIBUT

4 skinless halibut, cod, or other white flaky fish fillets (6 ounces each)

½ teaspoon kosher salt

½ teaspoon freshly ground black pepper

½ Fresno chile or jalapeño, thinly sliced

FOR SERVING

Chopped fresh cilantro

2 tablespoons toasted sesame seeds, optional

1 lime, cut into wedges

PAIRING SUGGESTION: Herby Rice Pilaf (page 200) or Sesame Asparagus Sauté (page 196)

MAKE THE WHITE WINE MISO SAUCE: In a small saucepan, combine the wine, coconut sugar, miso, coconut aminos, broth, lime juice, and ginger. Whisk over medium heat until smooth, about 2 minutes, breaking up the miso paste as you go. Bring to a simmer, stirring often, and cook for 3 to 4 minutes to allow the flavors to meld and for the sugar to dissolve. Remove from the heat and let cool before pouring over the fish.

COOK THE HALIBUT: Pat the halibut fillets dry and place them in a single layer in a baking dish. Spoon three-quarters of the miso sauce over the fillets, taking care not to touch the raw fish and then double-dip your spoon back in the sauce. You'll be using the rest of the sauce to top the fish once it is out of the oven. Season with the salt and pepper. Top with the jalapeño.

PLACE the halibut on the top rack of the oven and set it to broil. Broil until the fish flakes easily with a fork and is cooked through, 4 to 5 minutes.

SPOON the reserved miso sauce over the halibut. Garnish with cilantro and toasted sesame seeds (if using) and serve with lime wedges.

FROM MY KITCHEN TO YOURS

Have leftover miso paste? Try making the Harvest Salad with Miso Dressing (page 43) or the Spicy Miso Ramen with Pork (page 69).

Spicy Sichuan Fish

MAKES 4 SERVINGS • TOTAL TIME: 30 MINUTES

If you're a loyal blog reader, I'm sure you're well aware of the Snodgrass family's love of Sichuan peppercorns and Sichuan food. One of our favorite dishes to order when dining out is the Spicy Sichuan Fish that comes in a hot pot. The flavors are intense, and it's just one of those dishes that you simply cannot stop eating. It's absolutely delicious. I've done my best to bring those hot-pot flavors into an at-home skillet dinner, poaching the fish in a delightful spicy Sichuan broth. Ladled over rice, this is hands-down one of my favorite Sichuan-inspired dinners for a busy weeknight!

2 tablespoons avocado oil

2 celery stalks, cut into thin 2-inch-long matchsticks

4 green onions, halved lengthwise and cut into 2-inch lengths

4 dried Thai red chiles

1-inch piece fresh ginger, peeled and sliced into very thin matchsticks

2 garlic cloves, very thinly sliced

½ teaspoon kosher salt

½ teaspoon ground white pepper

2 tablespoons gochujang (I like Mother In Law's Fermented Chile Paste Concentrate; see note on page 85)

1 cup low-sodium seafood stock

¼ cup coconut aminos

1 teaspoon fish sauce

1 teaspoon rice vinegar

1 teaspoon Sichuan peppercorns

1½ pounds skinless halibut, cod, or salmon fillets, cut into 2-inch pieces

1 cup bean sprouts

2 tablespoons fresh cilantro leaves

Steamed white rice, optional for serving

IN a large deep saucepan, heat the oil over medium heat. Add the celery, green onions, Thai chiles, ginger, garlic, salt, and white pepper and cook, stirring often, until the vegetables are slightly tender, about 3 minutes. Add the gochujang, seafood stock, coconut aminos, fish sauce, and rice vinegar. Stir until well combined and bring to a boil. Reduce the heat to a simmer to let the flavors meld while you crush the peppercorns.

PLACE the Sichuan peppercorns in a plastic bag. Place under a heavy skillet and use a rocking motion to gently crush the peppercorns. Add the crushed peppercorns to the sauce. Carefully add the fish and bean sprouts and spoon the sauce over the fish to coat. Cover and cook at a simmer until the fish is just cooked through, 4 to 5 minutes.

TO SERVE: Spoon the sauce over the fish and garnish with cilantro. Serve over rice, if desired.

gimme all the sides

Parmesan-Roasted Zucchini

MAKES 4 SERVINGS • TOTAL TIME: 25 MINUTES

In my opinion, this is the best way to eat zucchini: super fast, healthy, and a little crispy—it always hits the spot! Coming together in 20 minutes, this roasted zucchini melts in your mouth, while the Parmesan adds a subtle salty crunch to liven up the flavor. This pairs well with just about anything, and my family always devours it in minutes!

2 large zucchini, trimmed and cut into ¼-inch-thick slices

3 tablespoons extra-virgin olive oil

½ teaspoon kosher salt

½ teaspoon freshly ground black pepper

½ teaspoon garlic powder

¼ cup freshly grated Parmesan cheese

PREHEAT the oven to 425°F. Line a large sheet pan with parchment paper.

PLACE the zucchini on the lined sheet pan and drizzle with the olive oil and season with the salt, pepper, and garlic powder. Toss until well combined. Spread the zucchini in an even layer and sprinkle with the Parmesan.

ROAST until golden brown and tender, about 20 minutes.

Sesame Asparagus Sauté

MAKES 4 SERVINGS • TOTAL TIME: 10 MINUTES

2 bunches asparagus, woody
ends trimmed, cut into 2-inch
pieces

2 tablespoons extra-virgin olive oil

2 garlic cloves, minced

Grated zest of ½ lemon

2 teaspoons white sesame seeds

½ teaspoon kosher salt

¼ teaspoon freshly ground black
pepper

1 tablespoon coconut aminos

We eat asparagus weekly at our house. I love how versatile it is; sometimes I simply roast it to serve alongside dinner, but other times I'll sauté it up like I've done here. This sesame seed—infused asparagus sauté is delicious with just about everything!

BRING a medium saucepan of water to a boil. Carefully add the asparagus to the boiling water and cook until crisp-tender, about 2 minutes.

MEANWHILE, in a skillet heat the oil over medium heat. Add the garlic, lemon zest, and sesame seeds and cook, stirring often, until the garlic is fragrant and the sesame seeds are lightly toasted, about 1 minute.

DRAIN the asparagus, transfer to the skillet, and add the salt and pepper. Increase the heat to medium-high and cook, stirring often, until the asparagus is lightly browned, about 3 minutes.

ADD the coconut aminos and stir until well combined. Continue to cook, stirring, until the sauce is slightly thickened and coats the asparagus, about 2 minutes.

Balsamic-Thyme Roasted Mushrooms

GLUTEN-FREE
DAIRY-FREE
PALEO
WHOLE30
GRAIN-FREE
VEGETARIAN

MAKES 4 SERVINGS • TOTAL TIME: 30 MINUTES

Roasted mushrooms make for a juicy and delectable side dish for practically any meal! They're beautiful and super easy to make. The mushrooms practically create their own pan sauce while roasting in the oven; at the end of the cook time, I simply thicken the liquid with a slurry to create an almost gravy-like sauce for the mushrooms to soak in. It's an impressive side dish with minimum effort—ideal!

2 pounds whole baby bella mushrooms

¼ cup extra-virgin olive oil

½ teaspoon Dijon mustard

¼ cup balsamic vinegar

1 tablespoon fresh thyme leaves, plus more for serving

1 teaspoon garlic powder

1 teaspoon kosher salt

½ teaspoon freshly ground black pepper

1 teaspoon arrowroot flour

Flaky salt, for serving

PREHEAT the oven to 425°F. Arrange the mushrooms in a 9 × 13-inch baking dish.

IN a medium bowl, whisk together the olive oil, mustard, vinegar, thyme, garlic powder, salt, and pepper until well combined.

POUR the balsamic mixture over the mushrooms and toss until well combined. Spread the mushrooms in an even layer and roast until golden brown and tender, about 18 minutes.

REMOVE the pan from the oven and set the oven to a high broil.

IN a small bowl, whisk the arrowroot flour and 1 tablespoon water. Pour the arrowroot mixture over the mushrooms and toss to combine.

BROIL until the sauce has thickened and the mushrooms are slightly charred, watching carefully, 2 to 3 minutes.

SPRINKLE with flaky salt. If desired, garnish with fresh thyme leaves.

Herby Rice Pilaf

MAKES 4 SERVINGS • TOTAL TIME: 30 MINUTES

This herby rice pilaf is really tasty and super versatile. Depending on what herbs you choose, it pairs well with just about everything! Use cilantro and pair it with my Ultimate Skillet Chicken Fajitas (page 149), Salmon al Pastor (page 176), or Herby Green Curry Poached Halibut (page 175). Or you can use my favorite combination of parsley and dill as I do below and serve it with Perfectly Broiled Rib Eye with Tarragon Butter (page 130), Steak au Poivre (page 112), or even Crispy Chicken Milanese with Arugula Salad (page 146). The possibilities are endless!

2 tablespoons avocado oil

1 cup minced yellow onion (about ½ medium onion)

2 garlic cloves, minced

Grated zest of ½ lemon

1 teaspoon kosher salt

1 cup white basmati rice

1½ cups low-sodium vegetable broth

1 cup chopped fresh herbs (half parsley and half dill is my favorite)

IN a large saucepan, heat the oil over medium heat. Add the onion, garlic, lemon zest, and salt and cook, stirring often, until the onion is tender, 4 to 5 minutes. Add the rice and cook, stirring often, to toast the rice, about 4 minutes. It will be fragrant and lightly browned.

ADD the broth and stir to combine. Bring the liquid to a boil, reduce the heat to a simmer, cover, and cook until the rice is tender and the liquid is absorbed, about 15 minutes.

REMOVE the rice from the heat and let it sit, covered, for 10 minutes. Add the herbs and fluff with a fork before serving.

Brothy Borracho Beans

GLUTEN-FREE
DAIRY-FREE

MAKES 8 SERVINGS • TOTAL TIME: 2 HOURS 30 MINUTES

Borracho beans (or frijoles borrachos *in Spanish, which translates to "drunken beans") are absolutely delicious simmered in a beer broth with bacon, onions, tomatoes, and spices. They do take some time to cook, but they'll leave your house smelling lovely. And don't be concerned—they won't leave you feeling woozy! I love making a batch of these at the beginning of the week to eat for lunch, but they're also great to serve to guests as an easy make-ahead side dish. This dish will become a part of your permanent rotation!*

6 slices bacon, cut into 1-inch pieces

2 cups diced yellow onion (about 1 large onion)

1 medium jalapeño, seeded and minced

2 garlic cloves, minced

1 pound dried pinto beans, presoaked (see note)

4 cups (32 ounces) low-sodium vegetable broth

12 ounces light beer

½ cup finely chopped seeded Roma (plum) tomato (about 1 tomato)

⅓ cup loosely packed finely chopped fresh cilantro leaves and tender stems

1 tablespoon chili powder

1 teaspoon smoked paprika

2 teaspoons garlic powder

1½ teaspoons ground cumin

1 teaspoon kosher salt, plus more to taste

½ teaspoon freshly ground black pepper

2 bay leaves

HEAT a large saucepan or Dutch oven over medium heat. Add the bacon and cook, stirring occasionally, until the bacon is browned and crisp around the edges, about 5 minutes. Add the onion, jalapeño, and garlic and cook, stirring often, until the onion is translucent and tender, about 5 minutes.

STIR in the beans, broth, beer, tomato, cilantro, chili powder, smoked paprika, garlic powder, cumin, salt, and black pepper. Bring to a boil over high heat, then reduce the heat to a light simmer, add the bay leaves, cover, and cook, stirring every 20 to 30 minutes, until the beans are tender, about 2 hours.

TASTE and add more salt as desired. Discard the bay leaves.

FROM MY KITCHEN TO YOURS

Soaking beans ahead of time helps them cook faster and more evenly, and it can also make them easier to digest. You can either soak the beans overnight or do a quick soak. To soak them overnight, throw the beans in a large bowl and cover with water by 2 inches. Let them soak for at least 4 hours or up to 12 hours. Drain and rinse before using. To quick soak, put the beans in a pot on the stove, cover with water by 2 inches, and bring to a boil. Remove from the heat and let soak for 1 hour. Drain and rinse, then proceed with the recipe.

Little Gem Salad with Lemon Dressing

MAKES 4 SERVINGS • TOTAL TIME: 10 MINUTES

This recipe uses one of those all-purpose salad dressings that pair well with almost any dish, and my mother always makes it when we dine at her house. It's a beautiful, bright, and tangy lemon dressing that I love to make at the beginning of the week and pour over any greens I have on hand to serve with dinner. But I love it best over Little Gem lettuce with sliced avocado to add a touch of creaminess and a little grated Parmesan on top for a bit of nuttiness. The dressing calls for a lot of extra-virgin olive oil, so for best results, be sure to select a great olive oil that you really love the taste of!

2 garlic cloves, peeled

½ teaspoon anchovy paste or 2 oil-packed anchovy filets

½ cup extra-virgin olive oil

¼ cup freshly squeezed lemon juice (about 2 lemons)

¼ teaspoon kosher salt, or to taste

¼ teaspoon freshly ground black pepper, or to taste

6 cups Little Gem lettuce, torn into leaves (or lettuce greens of your choice)

1 avocado, thinly sliced

¼ cup freshly grated Parmesan cheese (omit for dairy-free, paleo, and Whole30)

IN a food processor or blender, combine the garlic, anchovy paste, olive oil, lemon juice, salt, and pepper and blend until smooth.

PLACE the lettuce in a large serving bowl and pour the dressing on top. Toss until very well coated. Add the sliced avocado and gently toss once more. Top with the grated Parmesan and serve immediately.

FROM MY KITCHEN TO YOURS

This salad dressing keeps for 2 or 3 days, so it's great to prepare ahead of time to make your weeknight meal easier or to have one less task on the day of an event you're hosting.

Apple Cider Vinegar and Dijon Roasted Root Vegetables

GLUTEN-FREE
DAIRY-FREE
PALEO
WHOLE30
GRAIN-FREE
VEGETARIAN

MAKES 4 SERVINGS • TOTAL TIME: 40 MINUTES

These roasted root vegetables are quite frankly one of the best side dishes ever—they have a delicious flavor, and they pair well with a variety of dishes! First of all, root vegetables have a lot of natural sugars in them, which caramelize as they are roasted at a high temperature. What then sends these even more over the top is that they are tossed with strongly acidic apple cider vinegar, olive oil, fresh thyme, and Dijon to create an absolutely fantastic, flavorful side dish. While these are obviously great in the fall, I love this side dish so much it's a part of our dinner table year round!

3 tablespoons extra-virgin olive oil

¼ cup apple cider vinegar

1 tablespoon Dijon mustard

1 teaspoon dried thyme

1½ teaspoons kosher salt

2 large carrots, peeled and cut into 2-inch lengths

2 large parsnips, peeled and cut into 2-inch lengths

1 large sweet potato, peeled and cut into 2-inch-thick wedges

1 medium red onion, halved and cut into ½-inch-thick slices

PREHEAT the oven to 450°F. Line a large sheet pan with parchment paper.

IN a small bowl, whisk together the olive oil, apple cider vinegar, mustard, thyme, and salt. Place the carrots, parsnips, sweet potato, and onion on the prepared pan and drizzle with the apple cider vinegar mixture. Toss until the vegetables are evenly coated and spread the vegetables in an even layer.

ROAST until the vegetables are cooked through and golden brown on the edges, about 30 minutes.

Braised Brussels Sprouts

MAKES 4 SERVINGS • TOTAL TIME: 25 MINUTES

Brussels sprouts have suffered a bad reputation for decades—but when cooked properly, they taste absolutely fantastic! I love snagging a bag of presliced Brussels sprouts to use in recipes throughout the week. I once had a sudden craving for braised collard greens but only had Brussels sprouts on hand, so I decided to swap them into the recipe. To my surprise, they were a huge hit on my family table and have become a go-to side dish that pairs well with just about anything.

3 ounces diced pancetta

¼ cup diced shallot (about 1 large shallot)

2 garlic cloves, minced

¼ teaspoon crushed red pepper flakes

18 ounces shaved Brussels sprouts (see note)

3 tablespoons apple cider vinegar

¾ cup low-sodium vegetable or chicken broth

½ teaspoon kosher salt

½ teaspoon freshly ground black pepper

HEAT a large deep skillet over medium heat. Add the pancetta and cook, stirring often, until it begins to crisp, 3 to 5 minutes. Add the shallot, garlic, and pepper flakes and cook, stirring, until the shallots are just tender, about 2 minutes.

ADD the Brussels sprouts and vinegar and cook, stirring often, until the Brussels sprouts begin to wilt, about 2 minutes.

ADD the broth, salt, and black pepper and stir until well combined. Reduce the heat to medium-low, cover, and cook until the Brussels sprouts are very tender and the flavors have melded, about 10 minutes.

FROM MY KITCHEN TO YOURS

These days, most grocery stores sell preshredded Brussels sprouts in a bag. If you can't find them, it'll take you some extra time to shred them yourself, but the results are worth it. Slice off the bottom ½ inch of the sprouts and discard the outer leaves that fall off on their own. Use a very sharp knife or the slicing disc of a food processor to slice them really thin lengthwise.

1½ pounds large yellow potatoes, unpeeled, cut into 1-inch wedges

1½ teaspoons kosher salt

½ teaspoon freshly ground black pepper

½ teaspoon paprika

½ teaspoon garlic powder

⅛ teaspoon cayenne pepper, optional

3 tablespoons avocado oil

Zesty Potato Wedges

MAKES 4 SERVINGS • TOTAL TIME: 45 MINUTES

In this house, we love potatoes. Mashed, smashed, roasted, or fried, we are eating them! These roasted potato wedges are one of our favorite recipes. Roasting the potato wedges at a high temperature makes them soft and fluffy on the inside and perfectly crunchy on the outside, and the combination of spices adds a wonderfully addictive kick of flavor! These spices are also very versatile, making this side dish work with anything from my Juicy Indoor Burgers (page 133) to fish or steak! The potatoes are great as is, or you can serve them with your favorite dipping sauce, like ketchup or ranch.

PREHEAT the oven to 400°F. Line a large sheet pan with parchment paper.

PLACE the potato wedges on the lined sheet pan and season with the salt, pepper, paprika, garlic powder, and cayenne (if using). Toss until evenly coated. Add the oil and toss again until evenly coated. Spread the potatoes in a single layer in the pan so that none of them touch.

BAKE for 20 minutes, then turn the potatoes over and continue to bake until a deep golden-brown crust has formed, 10 to 15 minutes.

something
sweet

GLUTEN-FREE
VEGETARIAN

Scotcharoos

MAKES 18 TO 24 SQUARES • TOTAL TIME: ABOUT 1 HOUR 15 MINUTES

I have fond memories of these chewy, chocolate-covered rice cereal bars from when I was growing up. JoEllyn, the mom of one of my very best friends, made these for every event that I can think of, and I literally could not stop eating them! While they're certainly easy to make, nobody in town could make them as perfectly as JoEllyn—trust me. I've made some tweaks to her recipe here, but the flavor and nostalgia are still packed into every bite!

1 cup honey

1 cup creamy unsalted, unsweetened peanut butter

1 teaspoon pure vanilla extract

2 tablespoons avocado oil

6 cups brown rice crisp cereal (I use One Degree Organic Foods sprouted brown rice crisps; you can sub Rice Krispies if not gluten-free)

12 ounces butterscotch baking chips

8 ounces dark chocolate chips

½ teaspoon flaky salt, optional for topping

LINE a 9 × 13-inch baking dish with parchment paper, letting it hang over the two short sides of the pan (you'll use it to lift out the bars later).

IN a medium saucepan, heat the honey over medium heat and bring to a boil for just 1 minute. Remove from the heat and stir in the peanut butter, vanilla, and avocado oil until smooth.

POUR the peanut butter mixture into a large bowl and add the rice cereal. Stir until very well combined.

TRANSFER the mixture to the prepared baking dish and press into an even layer. Set aside to cool completely.

MEANWHILE, in a microwave-safe bowl, combine the butterscotch and dark chocolate chips. Microwave for 30 seconds, then carefully take the bowl out and stir. Repeat in 30-second increments until the mixture is completely melted and smooth, taking care not to overcook. In my microwave it takes about 2 minutes total.

POUR the chocolate-butterscotch mixture over the cereal in the pan and spread evenly. Sprinkle with the flaky salt, if using, and set aside to let cool completely (this takes a while to cool, at least 1 hour, but you have to let it completely cool before slicing or it won't hold together as well!). Using the edge of the parchment, lift the Scotcharoo block out of the baking dish and set it on a cutting board. Cut it into squares.

KEEP stored in an airtight container on the counter for up to 7 days or in the freezer for up to 3 months.

Lemon Avocado Oil Cake

MAKES 10 SLICES • TOTAL TIME: ABOUT 1 HOUR 15 MINUTES

GLUTEN-FREE
DAIRY-FREE
PALEO
GRAIN-FREE
VEGETARIAN

First off, if you've never had olive oil cake, you're missing out! It's a Mediterranean cake that's slightly sweet and finished with olive oil to add a subtle flavor while also helping to keep the cake moist. This lemon and avocado oil cake offers all the traditional subtleties, plus the twist of rosemary simple syrup. While the simple syrup can be omitted if you want a more traditional texture and taste, I highly recommend it for an added boost of flavor and moisture that will be sure to leave your guests impressed and making it perfect to eat throughout the week because who says cake can't be for breakfast?

FOR THE CAKE

Nonstick cooking spray

¾ cup avocado oil

3 large eggs

½ cup pure maple syrup

½ teaspoon pure vanilla extract

2 heaping tablespoons grated lemon zest (about 2 lemons)

⅔ cup freshly squeezed lemon juice, strained (about 3 lemons)

2¾ cups super-fine almond flour

½ cup tapioca flour

½ teaspoon kosher salt

1½ teaspoons baking powder

½ teaspoon baking soda

FOR THE ROSEMARY SIMPLE SYRUP

3 tablespoons water

2 tablespoons freshly squeezed lemon juice (about 1 lemon)

⅓ cup pure maple syrup

1 fresh rosemary sprig

OPTIONAL FOR SERVING

Whipped cream (I use So Delicious dairy-free coconut whipped cream)

1 grapefruit, peeled and cut into suprêmes (see note)

POSITION a rack in the center of the oven and preheat to 350°F. Set a 9-inch cake pan on a sheet of parchment paper, trace a circle onto the paper around the bottom of the pan, and cut out the paper round. Lightly spray the pan with the nonstick cooking spray, coating all the sides. Set the parchment round into the pan and press it in lightly to fit. Set aside.

IN a large bowl using a handheld mixer (or a stand mixer fitted with the whisk), beat the eggs on medium speed until pale yellow and frothy, 2 to 3 minutes. It's essential that you whip air into the eggs; this gives the cake volume. Slowly add the avocado oil, maple syrup, vanilla, lemon zest, and lemon juice. Beat until well combined.

IN a separate large bowl, whisk the almond flour, tapioca flour, salt, baking powder, and baking soda until well combined. In 1-cup increments on medium speed, slowly add the flour mixture to the wet ingredients, whisking well until smooth.

CAREFULLY pour the batter into the prepared pan, leaving ½ to ¾ inch of space from the top of the pan to prevent overflow in the oven. Tap the cake pan lightly on the counter to release any air bubbles.

BAKE until the cake is golden brown and a toothpick or cake tester inserted into the center of the cake comes out clean, 45 to 55 minutes. If the cake begins to brown too quickly, place a sheet of foil loosely over the top. Let the cake rest in the pan for 10 minutes.

MEANWHILE, MAKE THE ROSEMARY SIMPLE SYRUP: In a small saucepan, combine the water, lemon juice, maple syrup, and rosemary. Bring the mixture to a low boil over medium heat, whisking often, and cook for 4 minutes, to let the maple syrup reduce slightly and for the sugars to dissolve. Remove from the heat and let the rosemary steep in the syrup for at least 20 minutes before using. Discard the rosemary.

FROM MY KITCHEN TO YOURS

To make beautiful, juicy little grapefruit segments with no pith or skin, set the peeled grapefruit on a cutting board and use a thin, sharp knife to cut down the sides of the fruit, just through the remaining pith and membranes, to reveal the flesh underneath. Then, remove each segment of grapefruit by cutting along the sides of the segments to release them from the membranes, removing the seeds as you go.

USING a butter knife, carefully loosen the edges of the cake. Place a wire cooling rack over the pan and carefully flip the pan so that the top of the cake is resting on the rack. Carefully lift the pan from the cake, then remove the parchment. Using your hands or a sturdy spatula, carefully flip the cake a second time so it's no longer upside down on the rack.

LINE a sheet pan with parchment paper to catch the syrup drippings. Place the cooling rack with the cake on the lined sheet pan. Using a cake tester or toothpick, poke 20 to 25 holes in the cake to let the syrup soak through. Use a pastry brush to cover the cake with the syrup, making sure to get the top and sides.

TO SERVE the cake, transfer to a serving platter and cut with a serrated knife. Serve alone or topped with whipped cream and grapefruit suprêmes.

KEEP stored in an airtight container at room temperature for 4 to 6 days or frozen in an airtight container for up to 3 months.

Sutton's No-Bake Monster Cookie Bites

GLUTEN-FREE
VEGETARIAN

MAKES ABOUT 18 BITES • TOTAL TIME: 45 MINUTES

My daughters and I regularly make no-bake energy bites together. They're great to keep in the fridge for an afterschool snack, add a little extra oomph to breakfast, or serve as a fun treat in lunchboxes. But best of all, they're easy enough for my eight-year-old to make by herself, as long as I'm there to remind her of each step. I love seeing her confidently take charge of the recipe and get creative with what goes inside, but this monster cookie-inspired bite wins as the best combination in our home!

1¼ cup quick oats (I use Bob's Red Mill gluten-free quick-cooking rolled oats)

⅓ cup pure maple syrup

½ cup creamy unsalted, unsweetened almond butter

2 tablespoons chia seeds

1 teaspoon pure vanilla extract

¼ cup mini chocolate chips

¼ cup mini M&M's

2 tablespoons unsweetened shredded coconut

¼ teaspoon ground cinnamon

¼ teaspoon kosher salt

IN a large bowl, combine all the ingredients. Using a wooden spoon, stir until very well combined. Refrigerate for 30 minutes.

PORTION into bites of the desired size. I use a cookie scoop and roll mine into about 1-inch bites.

FROM MY KITCHEN TO YOURS

Keep stored in an airtight container in the refrigerator for up to 2 weeks or freeze them for up to 3 months. I love to keep them in the freezer and pop them into the kids' lunchboxes! If I pack them in the morning, by the time they get to lunch they are thawed out and ready to be eaten.

Individual Texas "Sheet" Cakes

MAKES 10 MINI CAKES • TOTAL TIME: 45 MINUTES

When I was growing up, especially in my high school years, my mom made an entire Texas sheet cake for me and my good friend once a week! This nostalgic chocolate cake recipe was made in a jelly-roll pan, which is simply a smaller version of a sheet pan, hence the name "sheet cake." I've tried and tried to make my mom's recipe using more wholesome ingredients, so when I finally got this recipe down, I was super excited. Now, I did switch the recipe to use a muffin tin to make individual-size cakes, because I've found that there's less room for error this way. Just trust me. The end result is fantastic, and it gives me all the lovely nostalgic vibes with every bite!

FOR THE MINI CAKES

Nonstick cooking spray

2 large eggs, at room temperature

⅓ cup coconut sugar

¼ cup pure maple syrup

¼ cup creamy unsalted, unsweetened cashew butter

2 tablespoons avocado oil

1 teaspoon pure vanilla extract

½ cup super-fine almond flour

⅓ cup unsweetened cocoa powder

1 teaspoon ground cinnamon

½ teaspoon baking soda

½ teaspoon baking powder

¼ teaspoon kosher salt

FOR THE ICING

⅓ cup pure maple syrup

2 tablespoons creamy unsalted, unsweetened cashew butter

1 tablespoon unsweetened cocoa powder

1 teaspoon arrowroot flour

3 tablespoons mini semisweet chocolate chips (for dairy-free, use Enjoy Life brand)

FOR THE TOPPING

¼ cup roughly chopped toasted pecans

Flaky salt, optional

POSITION a rack in the center of the oven and preheat the oven to 350°F. Mist 10 cups of a standard muffin tin with cooking spray.

MAKE THE CAKES: In a large bowl using a handheld mixer (or a stand mixer fitted with the whisk), beat the eggs for 2 to 3 minutes on medium speed until pale yellow and frothy. Add the coconut sugar, maple syrup, cashew butter, avocado oil, and vanilla and whisk until well combined.

IN a medium bowl, combine the almond flour, cocoa powder, cinnamon, baking soda, baking powder, and salt. Stir to mix well. Slowly add the flour mixture to the wet ingredients and beat on low until smooth and just combined. The batter should be between the thickness of brownie batter and that of pancake batter. Scoop about ¼ cup of the batter into each sprayed cup of the prepared muffin tin, filling it about halfway.

BAKE until a toothpick inserted into the center of a cake comes out clean, about 9 minutes. Remove from the oven and let cool in the pan for at least 10 minutes. When cooled, use a rubber spatula or butter knife to carefully loosen the edges of the cakes and transfer to a wire cooling rack. Place the mini cakes upside down on the rack and set aside while you prepare the icing.

MAKE THE ICING: In a small saucepan, combine the maple syrup, cashew butter, and cocoa powder. Bring to a simmer over low heat, whisking constantly, until well combined and slightly thickened, about 2 minutes.

IN a small bowl, combine the arrowroot flour and 1 tablespoon water. Whisk until well combined. While whisking, slowly pour the arrowroot mixture into the saucepan and whisk until the icing thickens, about 4 minutes.

REMOVE from the heat. Add the chocolate chips, and slowly whisk until combined and smooth. Let the icing cool slightly to let it thicken further, about 5 minutes.

LINE a sheet pan with parchment paper to catch the drippings. Place the rack with the upside-down cakes on the lined sheet pan. Once cooled, spoon about 1 tablespoon of the icing over each of the mini cakes and gently spread it out, letting it drip over the sides. Immediately top with chopped pecans and flaky sea salt (if using). Let the icing cool slightly on top of the cakes to help it adhere before serving, about 5 minutes.

KEEP stored in an airtight container on the counter for 4 to 5 days or in the freezer for up to 3 months.

7-Ingredient Almond Butter Cookies

MAKES 20 TO 24 COOKIES • TOTAL TIME: 20 MINUTES

I cannot resist these cookies! They're extremely easy to make, using only seven ingredients, and are a fan favorite over here in our household. You can use whatever nut butter you prefer or have on hand—I typically use smooth almond butter, but if you love peanut butter or another type of nut butter, then go for it! Just make sure your nut butter is unsweetened and natural, so it's thinner and easier to mix into the cookies. These have a soft and chewy center, slightly crisp edges, buttery bottoms, and a perfect amount of sweetness from the maple syrup. Heavenly.

1 cup creamy unsalted, unsweetened almond butter

¾ cup pure maple syrup

1 teaspoon pure vanilla extract

1½ cups super-fine almond flour

¼ cup arrowroot flour

½ teaspoon baking soda

½ teaspoon kosher salt

PREHEAT the oven to 350°F. Line two large sheet pans with parchment paper.

IN a large bowl, combine the almond butter, maple syrup, and vanilla and whisk until smooth. Add the almond flour, arrowroot flour, baking soda, and salt. Stir until just combined.

USING a small cookie scoop (about 2 teaspoons of dough per cookie), scoop the dough out and roll into balls. If needed, wet your hands a bit to keep the dough from sticking to them. Evenly space the cookie dough balls about 2 inches apart on the prepared sheet pans. You should get 20 to 24 cookies.

USING a fork, flatten the cookies slightly. Turn the fork 90 degrees and press down just slightly again to make a crosshatch pattern. If needed, wet the fork with warm water between each crisscross to keep it from sticking.

BAKE until golden brown on the edges but soft in the center, 8 to 9 minutes.

GENTLY bang the bottom of the pan on the countertop to help release any air pockets and to help them flatten further. Let the cookies cool on the sheet pan for 5 to 10 minutes; they will continue to cook a little from the residual heat and will be easier to remove.

KEEP stored in an airtight container at room temperature for 4 to 6 days or frozen in an airtight container or freezer bag for up to 3 months.

Birthday Cake Blondies

MAKES 16 BARS • TOTAL TIME: 35 MINUTES

These blondies are moist, chewy, and full of nostalgic birthday cake vibes! Filled with festive rainbow sprinkles and white chocolate chips, they're sure to brighten any day of the week! The blondies come together super quickly so they're perfect for when you need to throw something together in a pinch. I absolutely love making them with my girls, even though they always fight over who gets to add the sprinkles to the batter!

1 cup creamy unsalted, unsweetened almond butter or cashew butter

½ cup pure maple syrup

2 teaspoons pure vanilla extract

2 large eggs

1 tablespoon avocado oil

1 tablespoon super-fine almond flour

1 tablespoon arrowroot flour

½ teaspoon baking soda

¼ teaspoon kosher salt

1 cup dairy-free white chocolate chips (I like Lily's brand)

⅓ cup plus 1 tablespoon sprinkles (I like Supernatural brand)

PREHEAT the oven to 350°F. Line a 9 × 9-inch baking pan with parchment paper letting it hang over two sides of the pan (you'll use it to lift out the bars later).

IN a large bowl, combine the almond butter, maple syrup, vanilla, eggs, and avocado oil and stir until smooth. Add the almond flour, arrowroot flour, baking soda, and salt and stir until well combined. Fold in the white chocolate chips and ⅓ cup of sprinkles.

POUR into the prepared baking pan and spread into an even layer. Sprinkle the top with the remaining 1 tablespoon sprinkles.

BAKE until just cooked through and a toothpick inserted into the center comes out clean, about 20 minutes. Let cool in the pan. Using the edge of the parchment, lift the blondies out of the baking dish and set them on a cutting board. Cut into squares.

KEEP stored in an airtight container on the counter for up to 7 days or in the freezer for up to 3 months.

clayton's
cocktails

Tips and Tricks—Before You Sip!

HOW TO MAKE SIMPLE SYRUP

MAKES 1 CUP (8 OUNCES)

You'll notice a few of the recipes in this chapter call for simple syrup. While you can certainly buy it at a liquor store, it's a waste of money because you can easily make it at home—if you can boil water, you can make simple syrup! Here's how to do it.

1 cup water
1 cup sugar

IN a small saucepan, combine the sugar and water and bring to a simmer over medium-high heat. Stir until the sugar is dissolved, 3 to 4 minutes. Remove from the heat and let cool.

POUR the simple syrup into a jar and seal tightly with a lid.

SIMPLE syrup will keep in the refrigerator for up to 1 month. For a lower-calorie option, I recommend using monk fruit sweetener instead of sugar (*coconut sugar **does not** work!*). Just remember that monk fruit sweetener needs to be used immediately; it does not store well because it crystallizes.

WHY THE EGG WHITES?

There are a few cocktails in this chapter that call for egg whites. While it may seem like an odd addition for a drink, egg white is a pretty common ingredient in classic cocktails. Egg white produces that beautiful, pale layer of foam that you see on top of some drinks when dining out. Besides looking lovely, it adds a soft, pillowy element to the texture of drinks.

You may be intimidated when you see that a cocktail calls for an egg white, but those recipes are as easy as any other cocktail! You can either use fresh egg white, or out of the carton is fine, too. The one main difference when using egg whites in a cocktail is that it needs to be shaken without ice, also known as a "dry shake." This lets the egg emulsify and whip up. From there, you can pour the cocktail over ice. Please keep in mind that for vulnerable groups (including the elderly) it is suggested to avoid consumption of raw eggs because of the risk of salmonella.

WAIT TO ADD ICE TO YOUR SHAKER!

When measuring out your cocktails, don't put the ice in first! You'll just give the ice the opportunity to melt and water down your delightful cocktail. Measure your ingredients into the shaker, add the ice, and then shake it up.

Clayton's Margarita—3 Ways

MAKES 4 COCKTAILS

One of the most popular recipes on my blog year after year is Clayton's Margarita, and with good reason! This recipe has become an integral part of The Defined Dish as well as all our social gatherings with friends and family. While you can't go wrong with making the classic margarita recipe, we have a few simple twists to make your drinks even more exciting when you want a new flavor or festive twist!

CLAYTON'S CLASSIC MARGARITA

1 cup good tequila blanco

¼ cup Cointreau

½ cup freshly squeezed lime juice (about 4 limes)

½ cup Simple Syrup (page 228)

1 teaspoon egg white

Lime wedge and Tajín seasoning or kosher salt, for rimming the glass

CLAYTON'S GRAPEFRUIT MARGARITA

1 cup good tequila blanco

¼ cup Cointreau

¼ cup freshly squeezed grapefruit juice

¼ cup freshly squeezed lime juice (about 2 limes)

½ cup Simple Syrup (page 228)

1 teaspoon egg white

Lime wedge and Tajín seasoning or kosher salt, for rimming the glass

CLAYTON'S HOLIDAY MARGARITA

1 cup good tequila blanco

¼ cup Cointreau

¼ cup freshly squeezed lime juice (about 2 limes)

¼ cup pomegranate juice

½ cup Simple Syrup (page 228)

1 teaspoon egg white

Lime wedge and kosher salt, for rimming the glass

4 fresh rosemary sprigs, optional for serving

CHOOSE your margarita, then combine the tequila, Cointreau, juice(s), simple syrup, and egg white in a blender. Blend until frothy.

CUT a slit in the lime wedge and rub it along the rim of a glass. Roll the edge of the glass in the salt or Tajín to coat the rim. (Alternatively, you can opt to top the margarita itself with a sprinkle of Tajín or salt.) Carefully fill with ice and pour in the margarita. For the holiday version, garnish each glass with a sprig of rosemary, if desired. Enjoy!

FROM CLAYTON'S BAR TO YOURS

Clayton says he never stores his batch of margaritas in the fridge, as they tend to get too tart. He leaves the pitcher on the counter while people serve themselves. If the foam on top begins to disappear, simply blend again before pouring another round.

Espresso Martini

I'm an avid coffee drinker, and this is hands down one of my favorite cocktails. It's the perfect pick-me-up either to kick off the night or to sip on post-dinner instead of (or with) your dessert. While it does have a decent amount of alcohol in it, the coffee really masks that and makes it taste like a decadent treat, so be warned before you have a second serving!

3 ounces vodka (I use Tito's)
1 ounce Kahlúa
1 ounce Simple Syrup (page 228)
1½ ounces hot espresso

IN a cocktail shaker, combine the vodka, Kahlúa, simple syrup, and hot espresso. Fill with ice. Close, seal, and shake until very cold (at least 20 seconds).

PLACE a strainer on top of the shaker and pour the contents through a sieve (optional) directly into two glasses.

FROM CLAYTON'S BAR TO YOURS

It may seem strange to pour hot espresso into a cold drink, but the heat combined with the other ingredients in the cold shaker helps create the foam! While the sieve is not necessary, the strainer and the sieve together help to remove any tiny pieces of ice in your cocktail to create a rich, smooth froth.

Mezcal Mule

MAKES 2 COCKTAILS

The Moscow Mule is an incredibly popular cocktail. No matter the restaurant or bar, you're very likely to be able to order one. With its simple ingredients of vodka, ginger beer, and lime served in an icy copper mug, it's a total crowd-pleaser. Inspired by the original recipe, we've given it a smoky twist with this Mezcal Mule. It's a unique alternative that still offers plenty of familiar flavors for fans of the original cocktail!

6 fresh mint leaves, plus more for garnish

1½ ounces freshly squeezed lime juice (about 2 limes)

3 ounces mezcal

1½ ounces St. Germain elderflower liqueur

3 ounces ginger beer

Tajín seasoning, optional for garnish

IN a cocktail shaker, combine the mint leaves, lime juice, mezcal, and elderflower liqueur. Using a wooden cocktail muddler or wooden spoon, gently mash the mint 3 or 4 times to release the flavor. Fill the shaker with ice and shake until very cold (at least 20 seconds). Add the ginger beer to the shaker and gently stir to combine.

FILL 2 copper mugs or cocktail glasses with ice and strain the cocktail into the glasses. Garnish with sprigs of mint and a pinch of Tajín, if using.

The Last Word

MAKES 2 COCKTAILS

The Last Word is a classic cocktail that dates back to the Prohibition Era. It's one of Clayton's go-to cocktails and is my personal favorite gin cocktail. It's super simple to make, as all of the ingredients have the same measure, and it's a complete crowd-pleaser. Serve it in a fancy coupe, sit back, relax, and sip as this drink wows your guests.

3 ounces gin (preferably Hendrick's)

3 ounces Maraschino liqueur (preferably Luxardo)

3 ounces freshly squeezed lime juice (about 3 limes)

3 ounces green Chartreuse

2 Maraschino cherries (preferably Luxardo), for garnish

IN a cocktail shaker, combine the gin, liqueur, lime juice, and Chartreuse. Fill the shaker with ice and shake until very cold (at least 20 seconds). Strain into two coupe or martini glasses and garnish each with a cherry.

Thyme 75

MAKES 2 COCKTAILS

This French 75 variation has great depth—the addition of the thyme kicks it up a notch. I love serving this elegant cocktail as a festive brunch beverage or as an aperitif. It's a great cocktail for any time of the year and it pairs well with most anything!

3 ounces gin (preferably Hendrick's)

2 ounces freshly squeezed lemon juice (about 1 lemon)

2 ounces thyme simple syrup (see note)

Brut Cava, to top

2 fresh thyme sprigs, for garnish

IN a cocktail shaker, combine the gin, lemon juice, and thyme simple syrup. Fill the shaker with ice and shake until very cold (at least 20 seconds). Strain into two coupe glasses (preferably chilled) and top with Cava. Garnish each with a sprig of thyme.

FROM CLAYTON'S BAR TO YOURS

To make the thyme simple syrup, make 1 cup of Simple Syrup (page 228). When you remove it from the heat, add 10 to 12 thyme sprigs, set aside, and let cool to room temperature, about 30 minutes. Remove and discard the thyme sprigs. Store in an airtight container in the refrigerator for up to 2 weeks.

Whiskey Sour

MAKES 2 COCKTAILS

This whiskey sour recipe has all the right proportions. It embraces the classic bright lemon flavor with the warming whiskey and offers a sweet note from simple syrup and elderflower liqueur. Whether you're a whiskey drinker or not, this cocktail goes down smoothly—sometimes too smoothly. Cheers!

4 ounces bourbon

½ ounce Simple Syrup (page 228)

1½ ounces freshly squeezed lemon juice (about ½ lemon)

1 ounce St. Germain elderflower liqueur

1 teaspoon egg white

2 Maraschino cherries (preferably Luxardo), for garnish

IN a cocktail shaker, combine the bourbon, simple syrup, lemon juice, elderflower liqueur, and egg white. Cover and dry shake (without ice) for 15 to 20 seconds. Serve over ice in an old fashioned glass. Garnish each with a cherry.

Golden Hour

MAKES 2 COCKTAILS

Named after one of my favorite Kacey Musgraves songs, this is a delicious cocktail to sip on during that afternoon "golden hour" time of the day—aka happy hour—while enjoying good music and delicious appetizers with the ones you love most. This lovely Aperol cocktail is brightened by lemon but given a touch of earthiness by an herb garnish. And, just as in the song, you'll know "Everything's gonna be alright" when you're sipping on this!

4 ounces vodka (I use Tito's)

2 ounces St. Germain elderflower liqueur

2 ounces Aperol

2 ounces freshly squeezed lemon juice (about 1 lemon)

Topo Chico or club soda

Fresh rosemary, thyme, or mint sprigs, for garnish

IN a cocktail shaker, combine the vodka, elderflower liqueur, Aperol, and lemon juice. Fill the shaker with ice and shake until very cold (at least 20 seconds). Strain into two old-fashioned glasses filled with ice and top off with Topo Chico. Garnish with an herb of your choice.

back to basics

Fauxtisserie Chicken (Instant Pot and Slow Cooker Methods)

GLUTEN-FREE
DAIRY-FREE
PALEO
WHOLE30
GRAIN-FREE

MAKES 4 SERVINGS • TOTAL TIME: 45 MINUTES

Throughout this book, there are recipes that call for cooked, shredded or cubed chicken. You can certainly save on time and splurge on a store-bought rotisserie chicken; however, making your own faux rotisserie chicken at home is easy to do. Prepping this over the weekend and having it on hand to throw into soups, salads, and other recipes is a great way to save your energy throughout the week in the kitchen!

1 whole chicken (3½ to 4 pounds), giblets removed

1 lemon, quartered

1½ teaspoons kosher salt

½ teaspoon freshly ground black pepper

1 teaspoon paprika

1 teaspoon garlic powder

½ teaspoon onion powder

1 teaspoon dried oregano

2 cups (16 ounces) low-sodium chicken broth

PAT the chicken skin dry. Place the lemon quarters inside the cavity. In a small bowl, combine the salt, pepper, paprika, garlic powder, onion powder, and dried oregano. Coat the chicken all over with the spice mixture.

INSTANT POT METHOD

PREPARE the chicken as directed above.

PLACE the steamer rack in the bottom of the Instant Pot. Pour the chicken broth into the pot and place the chicken on the steamer rack. Close the lid, turn the valve to seal, and cook on high pressure for 25 minutes.

WHEN the cook time is complete, turn the valve to release the pressure. Once all the pressure is released and there is no remaining steam, carefully open the lid.

SLOW COOKER METHOD

PREPARE the chicken as directed above.

PLACE four 3-inch round balls of foil in the slow cooker to create a "rack" for the chicken to cook on. Place the chicken on top of the "rack" and pour the broth around the chicken. Cover and cook on high for 4 to 5 hours or on low for 8 to 10 hours. The chicken should be cooked through and have an internal temperature of 165°F.

FROM MY KITCHEN TO YOURS

To get crispy skin, preheat your oven's broiler to high and place the chicken on a rimmed sheet pan. Drizzle the chicken with olive oil. Broil until the skin has crisped to your liking, watching carefully so as not to burn the chicken, 2 to 4 minutes.

Quick-Pickled Red Onions

MAKES 4 SERVINGS • TOTAL TIME: 40 MINUTES

Want to jazz up a dish? Pickled red onions are a great way to give it a bright pop of flavor! Not only are they bright pink and gorgeous, they're tangy and add a little crunch, too. While I love adding them to tacos, salads, and bowls, they're also a great addition to dishes like the Salmon al Pastor (page 176) and Fried Avocado Tacos (page 96).

1 small red onion, halved and thinly sliced

¾ cup apple cider vinegar

½ teaspoon kosher salt

½ teaspoon black peppercorns

½ teaspoon coriander seeds

PLACE the sliced onion in a large bowl and cover with hot water. Let sit for 5 minutes (this takes the bite out of the onion).

MEANWHILE, in a medium bowl, whisk the vinegar, salt, peppercorns, and coriander seeds until all the salt has dissolved.

DRAIN the onion and place it in the vinegar mixture. Stir until well combined, cover (or transfer to an airtight container or jar), and transfer to the fridge to chill before serving, at least 30 minutes.

FROM MY KITCHEN TO YOURS

While these can be kept in the fridge for up to 2 weeks, I prefer to use mine within the first week.

Homemade Mayo

MAKES 1 CUP • TOTAL TIME: 1 MINUTE

If you've still never tried homemade mayo, you're in for a treat. It's ultracreamy and so much tastier than store-bought mayo! While you can add the optional ingredients (see below) and make yourself a typical mayo spread for sandwiches and beyond, I like to keep it simple and just make the emulsification base, ready to transform into creamy dressings like a creamy chipotle dressing (see Chopped Chipotle Chicken Salad, page 40), a Caesar dressing (see Buffalo Caesar Bowls, page 32), and Thai basil Green Goddess (see Chicken Paillard Salad, page 35). It's also magical in the tangy green sauce for Peruvian-Inspired Whole Roasted Chicken (page 156).

1 cup avocado oil or other light-flavored oil

1 large egg

OPTIONAL

1 garlic clove, minced

1 teaspoon freshly squeezed lemon juice

2 teaspoons mustard powder

Kosher salt, to taste

POUR the oil into a wide-mouth glass jar with an opening a little bit wider than the head of your immersion blender. Crack the egg into the oil and let it settle on the bottom of the jar.

PLACE the immersion blender in the jar and position the blade directly over the egg yolk. Turn the immersion blender on low and hold in place, with the blender running, until the ingredients at the bottom of the jar start to turn into a creamy emulsion, about 10 seconds.

START lifting the blender up a bit and pressing it back down, bringing the mixture above the mayo at the bottom into the emulsion, bit by bit, until you reach the top and the entire jar is emulsified.

USE this simple emulsification when I call for "homemade mayo" in the recipes throughout this book. Or you can turn it into a more traditional mayonnaise by blending in the optional ingredients.

acknowledgments

Writing a book takes a village, and my heart is filled with so much gratitude to the wonderful people who were involved in this crazy process and to my friends, family, and community who have supported me along the way.

First and foremost, a huge thank-you to the Defined Dish community; this book really is for you. I wouldn't be able to do what I do without your continued support and love along the way. It is my biggest hope that you cook through this book and enjoy special moments around the table with the ones you love most. Thank you for your support and enthusiasm that have allowed me to continue doing this dream job. I love you so much.

To my director of operations, Cady Grable: Everybody we meet wants a "Cady" in their life, and I'm just grateful to be the lucky one who has you in mine, because you really are one in a million. My life and this book would be a hot mess without you, and I thank you so much for the hard work and dedication you put into your job each day.

To my agent, Nicole Tourtelot: I am beyond grateful to have you in my corner and for always having my back. Thank you for always listening to me, calming my nerves, and helping me navigate the crazy process of making this book come to life. You are a real rock star.

And to the insanely creative and amazing team that brought this whole book to life through a pandemic and during

Texas's biggest ice storm—thank you, thank you, thank you! Where do I even begin? Even when I am old and gray, there is no way I will ever forget the memories we made during those wild two weeks.

Taylor Herz: Cooking in the kitchen with you makes my heart so happy, and I will always have fond memories of developing these recipes with you. Thank you for your love and support, and for always believing in me.

Judy Kim: Your eye for food styling and creativity is unparalleled, and I am so dang happy that you were a part of this book, because it turned out to be more beautiful than I could have ever dreamed! You are one incredibly talented woman, and I am in awe of your hard work, patience, creativity, and brilliant mind.

Kristen Kilpatrick: You have a way of bringing so much joy everywhere you go. I am so lucky that I get to work with you and call you my friend. Thank you for your patience and flexibility in working with me. I can always count on you to make magic happen, and I love you!

Nikki Pensabene: You are a bright light overflowing with good vibes and positivity, and I hope to be "mising" with you in the kitchen again sooner than later.

Lauren Withrow: Thank you for the adventurous spirit that you brought to set each day. You have a beautiful heart and are so incredibly talented, and I am so happy you were a part of this book.

McKenzie Mitchell: You are the best recipe tester ever, and I am so glad we met through the world of social media and are able to continue to work together. Thank you for all your hard work behind the scenes!

To my editor, Cassie Jones: Thank you for believing in my food and style of cooking. You have been a delight to work with as I try to navigate this book creation process, and your feedback is invaluable. And to the rest of the wonderful team at William Morrow—thank you for your enthusiastic determination to get this book published.

To Melissa Urban: I am still so grateful for what the Whole30 program has done for my life. Thank you for teaching me the importance of community, reading food labels, and listening to my body, for encouraging me to find my own "food freedom," and for endorsing my first cookbook. I owe so much of my success to the Whole30 program and community and appreciate you more than you know.

Denise Hernandez: Thank you for being the most supportive manager and for always listening to me and shouldering my anxieties. You are such a big part of this journey with me, and I am so thankful to have you by my side to stand up for me along the way.

Mom and Dad: Thank you for supporting me and loving me endlessly. Mom, you have taught me so much in the kitchen, and so many of these recipes are inspired by the fond memories we made together in the kitchen.

To my sister and best friend, Madison: What would I do without you? Every day I thank God that you are in my life. You are always there for me to support me in every way, and spending time with you always brings me peace and comfort. I love you.

To GoGo: Having you in my life immediately reduces my level of stress and anxiety. It's amazing to have a mother-in-law who is always on speed dial to help me. Thank you for your nonstop love, support, and friendship.

To Martha: I feel so lucky to have you in my life. Thank you for your constant support, for the love and care you give to me and the girls, and for your honest feedback on all the recipes I create in the kitchen.

To Clay, Caleb, Nathan, Kellye, and PaPa: Thank you for every single person that you tell about my book and my blog. I am so appreciative of the love and support you continue to give me, and I love you.

To my beautiful nieces and nephew, Temple, Bobbie, Fairlee, and Rex: I can't wait to watch you grow and cook with you in the kitchen. You are so loved.

To Charlie and Melissa: Thank you for braving the winter storm to be the most amazing glam squad. You always know how to make me feel beautiful and I am so glad to call you both my friends.

To my friends near and far, you know who you are: Thank you for not sticking me in a time capsule, because if you did I wouldn't be where I am today. Thank you for supporting me, allowing me to grow, and loving me along the way. Getting recipe texts from you means more to me than you'll ever know, and I am beyond grateful to have each of you in my life.

To my incredible husband, Clayton: You are my rock and my favorite taste tester in the whole world. Thank you for keeping me grounded and sane and for always standing up for me and believing in me even when I'm not believing in myself. I love you more than words can express.

And to my beautiful, fun, loving, and kind daughters, Sutton and Winnie: You are my everything, and I am so proud to be your mom. Cooking with you in the kitchen brings me more joy than you'll ever know. My hope is that you'll cook these recipes for the ones you love most and continue to spread joy everywhere you go. I love you.

Universal Conversion Chart

OVEN TEMPERATURE EQUIVALENTS

250°F = 120°C

275°F = 135°C

300°F = 150°C

325°F = 160°C

350°F = 180°C

375°F = 190°C

400°F = 200°C

425°F = 220°C

450°F = 230°C

475°F = 240°C

500°F = 260°C

MEASUREMENT EQUIVALENTS

Measurements should always be level unless directed otherwise.

⅛ teaspoon = 0.5 mL

¼ teaspoon = 1 mL

½ teaspoon = 2 mL

1 teaspoon = 5 mL

1 tablespoon = 3 teaspoons = ½ fluid ounce = 15 mL

2 tablespoons = ⅛ cup = 1 fluid ounce = 30 mL

4 tablespoons = ¼ cup = 2 fluid ounces = 60 mL

5⅓ tablespoons = ⅓ cup = 3 fluid ounces = 80 mL

8 tablespoons = ½ cup = 4 fluid ounces = 120 mL

10⅔ tablespoons = ⅔ cup = 5 fluid ounces = 160 mL

12 tablespoons = ¾ cup = 6 fluid ounces = 180 mL

16 tablespoons = 1 cup = 8 fluid ounces = 240 mL

index

NOTE: Page references in *italics* indicate photographs.

HarperCollins books may be purchased for educational, business, or sales promotional use. For information, please email the Special Markets Department at SPsales@harpercollins.com.

FIRST EDITION

Designed by Renata De Oliveira
Photography by Kristen Kilpatrick
Food styling by Judy Kim

Library of Congress Cataloging-in-Publication Data

Names: Snodgrass, Alex, author.
Title: The comfortable kitchen : 105 laid-back, healthy, and wholesome recipes / Alex Snodgrass.
Description: First edition. | New York : William Morrow, [2021] | Includes index. | Summary: "The New York Times bestselling author of The Defined Dish redefines comfort food with these simple, quick, and healthy weeknight dinners"—Provided by publisher.
Identifiers: LCCN 2021042640 | ISBN 9780063075412 (hardcover) | ISBN 9780063075474 (ebook)
Subjects: LCSH: Comfort food. | LCGFT: Cookbooks.
Classification: LCC TX714 .S5977 2021 | DDC 641.3—dc23
LC record available at https://lccn.loc.gov/2021042640

ISBN 978-0-06-307541-2

21 22 23 24 25 LSC 10 9 8 7 6 5 4 3 2 1